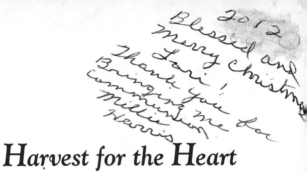

*Blessed and
Merry Christmas
Lori!
Thank you
bringing me to
communion
Millie
Harris*

Harvest for the Heart

Richard Gribble, CSC

✓ S0-CIG-770

BOOKS & MEDIA

BOSTON

ISBN 0-8198-3376-2

Cover photo: FSP
Cover design: Helen Rita Lane, FSP

Printed and published in the U.S.A. by Pauline Books and Media, 50 St. Paul's Avenue, Boston, MA 02130.

Pauline Books & Media is the publishing house of the Daughters of St. Paul, an international congregation of women religious serving the Church with the communications media.

1 2 3 4   99 98 97 96

Dedication

This book of reflections is dedicated to the person who inspired them—my best friend Mary. She has shown me the way to love others and live life. She has inspired me and encouraged me to produce this work. Her spirit permeates these pages.

Table of Contents

Introduction

Of all the relationships that we enjoy in this world, our relationship with God is both the most private and the most valued. We exercise our relationship with God, our best friend, in many varied ways each day. Our daily walk with the Lord leads us to that conversation we call prayer. We both speak with and listen to God. Each day we also work in the vineyard, called by baptism to minister to God's people. Our relationship with God is played out in the ecstasies of life, as well as its sorrows and defeats. As sinful and broken people we reach out each day to discover and enjoy the special presence of God in our lives.

The reflections in this volume come from the spirit of my daily search for and walk with Jesus. They reflect many moods and many different situations. These short responses to my interaction with God were written over a long period of time. Some were written on retreat when silence has more time to penetrate the soul and calm the noise of our active lives.

Others were written after a reading of God's word. Some of these reflections were written in response to the beauty of the day, as a thanksgiving for God's countless gifts, or to articulate the feelings that I had at any particular moment.

The human hunger for God can only be satisfied when we behold the beatific vision when God calls us home. Along the road of life, however, our hunger is daily satisfied by the experiences that come our way. Our hunger is not for food to nourish our bodies, but for that which satisfies our heart and soul. These reflections are independent experiences of faith which together form a harvest for the heart, which daily yearns for God.

It is impossible for all of these writings to speak to every person each day. Depending on your mood, perceived need, and what God tells you in your daily walk, the reflections that follow will touch each person in a different way. I hope that the reader will be touched in some way by these writings. If these reflections provide a vehicle for your own prayer life and a better insight into God, then they have served their purpose. This book is my way of sharing all the beauty that God has given to me.

Richard Gribble, CSC

God Walks with Us

Today Brings God's Gifts to Me

Today dawned warm and bright; it came as God's gift. I strolled along the sidewalk lined with cherry trees bursting into blossom. An occasional squirrel scurried across my path while the gentle breeze cooled the sun's warming rays. Beauty glistened all around me and God held me near.

Today's Mass inspired me. A missionary preached and his words fired me with the warmth of God's love. "We struggle to break the chains that bind us," he said, "but only God can release us." God reached out to me through the music, the people and the atmosphere.

The train whisked me to the city where traffic blared and people rushed through the streets. The commotion fascinated me. I decided to walk in order to enjoy the beautiful day, and took the short cut which curved along the bay. The breeze began to gust and it cooled the warmth of the sun's penetrating rays. Many people roamed along the waterfront. Joggers ran by and bicyclists and roller skaters swept past me. In the harbor, a navy vessel and a luxury liner swayed in the wind as water lapped against their hulls.

I sauntered to the edge of one pier. Clouds sailed through the clear sky and the wind buffeted against me. Boats churned through the choppy waters. I sat down and drank in the magnificent scene. It was God's gift to me.

I wandered down the roads again, climbing up steep hills and then down curvy roads. One panhandler begged for change while a drunk snored in the corner. The buses and trolleys rumbled through the streets, causing a din and spewing out black exhaust. But the excitement of the city thrilled me.

The concert enchanted me in a way that Mozart would have enjoyed. The violins played melodically as the brass and percussion pounded out their notes. The music added to the day's bounty.

At home that night, I relaxed and pondered the day. The sun had warmed me and the wind had chilled me. I had marveled at the beauty of nature and had heard the hubbub of the city and the melodies of the symphony. I had walked and had traveled by train. In all, I had been loved, for today truly brought God's gifts to me.

Hospitality—Showing
the Face of God to Others

Our busy world seems to intrude on our entire day. We rush to work in order to make a living for ourselves and our dependents. We wolf down our meals to get the nourishment we need. We hurry to ball fields, to the bank, to the supermarket and to the mall. Constantly on the move, we can't find time for ourselves, much less for others.

What happens when events and especially people interrupt our busy schedule? What do we do when others ask for our time and attention? All too often we refuse to stop. To stop interrupts us. It forces us to change our plans and go out of our way for someone else.

Scripture shows us the benefits of being hospitable to those who interrupt our life. The prophet Elijah wandered through Israel. Undoubtedly he interrupted many people. God sent him to do the work of the kingdom. Elijah had no place to stay, so he depended on others. One time in his travels, he came upon a widow and her son. He asked for bread and drink, but the widow hesitated. She had only enough flour and oil to prepare one meal for herself and her son. When that was gone, they would die, having nothing else to eat. But Elijah persisted and the woman provided for him. Elijah did not forget her. He promised her that through the power of God, the flour and oil would not run dry until rain came to water the earth. God rewarded that woman's hospitality.

People come into our lives asking for our time and resources, sometimes daily. Some need food, some a sympathetic ear and some only need love. We must respond to them generously as the widow of Zarephath did (cf. 1 Kgs 17:7-16). Just as God rewarded her, we too will find our reward. It may come in the form of a smile, a thank you, or a note of appreciation. But our recompense will come especially in the form of that wonderful feeling deep down inside each one of us. We need nothing else. When we help others, we might be surprised at what will happen, for the Letter to the Hebrews tells us, "Do not neglect to show hospitality to strangers, for thereby some have entertained angels unawares" (13:2). Let us welcome those whom God sends into our lives, even those who interrupt us, and we will find God's reward in the process.

Faith Shows the Way to God

The Letter to the Hebrews gives us a wonderful definition of faith. It states, "Faith is the assurance of things hoped for, the conviction of things not seen" (11:1). Faith invites us to think positively about the future and to believe what we cannot see.

The classic passage in the New Testament which teaches about faith is the story of Thomas (cf. Jn 20:19-29). The apostles had huddled together for fear of the Jewish authorities. Jesus came and stood before them. "Peace be with you," he said. The disciples rejoiced to see the Lord. Because he had not been present at Jesus' appearance, Thomas refused to believe it. He demanded physical proof, since he would not believe without seeing. One week later, the apostles had gathered together again, with Thomas present. Jesus appeared and greeted them, "Peace be with you." He chastised Thomas for failing to believe. Thomas could only cry out, "My Lord and my God."

Faith opens the door to the eternity which is God. God gifts us with faith, but we must exercise that gift in order for faith to flower and blossom forth. We exercise our faith by believing in that which seems impossible to us, which we can't understand. It seemed impossible at one time that humans could fly but now people don't give air travel a second thought. It seemed impossible that medicine could eradicate polio, but now it is virtually non-existent. If mysteries of the natural order can elude us, how much less can we grasp the things of God.

Faith shows us the way to God, if we can only follow. In his Second Letter to the Corinthians, St. Paul wrote beautifully, "We walk by faith, not by sight" (5:7). Sight allows us to see our world and to enjoy the sunrise and the beauty of God's creation. But we must walk with the eyes of faith in order to find that elusive yet free gift, eternal life. Without faith, that is, believing in what seems impossible to us, our lives dry up.

We can't comprehend that God became human. But with faith, we can not only believe in the Incarnation, we can also know that our God died so that we could have life. Let us live the life of God and show our faith. If we do, then the impossible becomes real and we find the road to salvation.

Faith Conquers Fear

Fear lurks all around us. We needn't look far to find it. Gangs and drug lords terrorize our city streets. The shadow of war constantly looms over our world. International terrorism promises to increase. Economic recession threatens to put us out of work or ruin our future plans. It's no wonder that in a world which has seemingly gone mad, people fear for their well-being.

But we have a solution to this fear which engulfs us. Faith gives us the answer. One might think that the opposite of fear is courage or bravery. But Scripture tells us that faith conquers fear.

St. Mark describes how Jesus dealt with fear (cf. Mk 4:35-41). Jesus and his disciples were sailing on the Sea of Galilee when a storm arose. Asleep on a cushion in the stern, Jesus seemed oblivious to the danger. The storm terrified the apostles and they cried out to Jesus. What did the Lord tell them? "Why are you afraid? Have you no faith?" Jesus did not ask for fortitude or perseverance. He asked only for faith.

Just as faith eased the disciples' fear, it can calm our fears as well. If we have faith in our abilities to work and act, then we can overcome all. If we have faith in our community and its leaders, then legislation can break the back of fear. If we have faith in God, then we can do all things with his help.

We must live in the world as it is, with all its troubles and tensions. Fear will not disappear, yet we can conquer it with the power of faith and the help of God.

Love Demands Commitment

During the turbulent 1960's a popular song stated, "Love is just a four-letter word." It implied that love is simple and floats into our lives without effort. Yet we know what difficult demands love can make, and how lucky we are to find someone we can love.

The word "love" can comprise the thoughts and feelings of a lifetime. We use the word so glibly. But what do we mean when we say "I love you?" Hopefully we mean that we dedicate ourselves completely to our loved one, united in thoughts and feelings. Love has various degrees and aspects. But a true love relationship demands commitment.

Commitment calls us to cast our lot with another. Commitment means that despite all difficulties, an unbreakable bond will always unite two people. The romantic love which books, television and movies have idolized is much more than a four-letter word. The Greeks used the term *eros* for romantic love, meaning that the bond between people is permanent and calls for full, complete and unconditional dedication.

A world full of problems and hate cries out for love. But we must realize that love goes beyond platitudes, kind words and nice gestures. Love claims a complete commitment to another, no matter what conditions or circumstances that life might throw our way. God loves us with unconditional love. We must learn to love others in a similar manner. If we can imitate God's love, then we will help build the kingdom of God on earth and come to eternal life as well.

Seeking God Our Rock

Tension crops up all around us—tension between the plastic and the solid, the make-believe and the real, the temporary and the permanent. We live in a world which stresses the here and now and accents what can be seen and handled. Our society craves this convenience and thrives on throwing things away. We can go to McDonald's without having to get out of the car—just drive through. We use disposable diapers, plates, razors and even cameras! At times, even people seem disposable.

Scripture challenges this prevailing attitude of a throwaway society that finds everything expendable. As St. Paul wrote, "We look not to the things that are seen but to the things that are unseen, for the things that are seen are transient, but the things that are unseen are eternal" (2 Cor 4:18). St. Paul realized that the world misjudges the temporary. To find our way, a way that leads to salvation, we must look to God as the rock of our lives.

We need not look far to find the tension between the temporary and the permanent. For example, tension exists between law and faith. The law is a good thing and keeps our society organized. Our world would fall into chaos without the law. Yet law changes and doesn't last forever. Instead, faith keeps on growing and always remains with us. That is why St. Paul said so often that faith justifies us, not observance of the law.

Tension also arises between our needs for relaxation and the needs of the community. People like to enjoy themselves. We need recreation in our lives, otherwise a total emphasis on work will dull us. But we must ask ourselves if we live only for fun. Are our lives a series of thrills from one excitement to the next? If so, what happens to community? Fun fades quickly, but community lasts forever, especially the community of faith. If we stay committed to each other through community, then we live in the permanent and come closer to God.

To contrast friends and relationships with our relationship to God also illustrates the tension between the temporary and the permanent. Friends come and go. We are fortunate if we have two or three lifelong friends with whom we can share ourselves. Relationships are important. They help us to see the face of God through others. But no matter how necessary and beautiful friends and relationships are, they are temporary. Only God endures forever. God always remains with us as the friend to whom we can always turn in trust.

We live in a fast-paced, frenetic world. The temporary screams out for our attention in varied ways. The law, enjoyments, and friends enrich our lives and can help to bring us to wholeness. Yet it is faith, community and God which bring us to salvation and eternal life. As St. Paul says, the temporary comes from the earth and will not last. The permanent comes from God and it will last forever and bring us to eternal life.

God Calls Us

"Go, therefore, and make disciples of all nations, baptizing them in the name of the Father and of the Son and of the Holy Spirit" (Mt 28:19). Jesus exhorted his disciples to spread the faith. He directs that call to us as well. Through baptism, the Lord summons us by name to go forth and actively pursue the call of God. He invites us to live a life of faith and holiness.

God sometimes breaks in on our lives at the most inopportune moment. When God called Amos, he responded that he was a shepherd, a dresser of sycamores. He was no prophet; he didn't want the job. Yet God commanded, "Go, prophesy to my people" (Amos 7:12). Amos obeyed and preached God's word. The young man in Matthew's Gospel ran to Jesus, telling the Lord that he wanted to follow him. The young man only asked to bury his father. But Jesus replied, "Leave the dead to bury their own dead" (Mt 8:22). Obviously, God's call makes demands.

God asks us to go forth and actively pursue the invitation to holiness. This call is never passive but asks something of us. Our Christian vocation springs from Baptism, but God beckons us in many ways each day. Opportunities to serve and minister to others surround us. If we sit back and do nothing, if we allow others around us to do the work, then we miss our call. Even more, we miss the opportunity of a lifetime to show the face of Christ to others.

We might ask, "What is the call?" St. Paul put it beautifully when he said that we are to take all in heaven and earth and make it one with Jesus as the head. God's plan is "to unite all things in him [Christ], things in heaven and things on earth" (Eph 1:10). But this task challenges us. We all need to respond to it by actively pursuing God's invitation to holiness. The call comes in different ways for each one, and requires our personal commitment.

God invites us. Do we listen? Jesus urged the disciples, and he urges us, to preach the word and cure the sick (cf. Mk 6:7-13). We can do it in faith for Jesus has assured us, "I am with you always" (Mt 28:20b).

Thy Will Be Done

During the loneliest and most desolate time in Jesus' life he prayed, "My Father, if this [cup] cannot pass unless I drink it, your will be done" (Mt 26:42b). All of us experience our personal "agony in the garden." For some, it comes as a specific trial, but many find the agony in life itself, in the daily struggle to live the Christian message. The incarnate God, Jesus Christ, offered his suffering and his will to the Father. So should we who profess the name of Christian.

Our twentieth century Western society focuses on the needs of the individual. We can forget about God's will in our lives. In his humanity, Jesus suffered the pain of abandonment. His fear of impending suffering and death, coupled with his complete submission to the Father's will gave us the perfect example of obedience. As a human being, Jesus did not desire death. Yet he desired to follow the Father's will and so he prayed, "Your will be done." Jesus' obedience to the will of God stands as a lesson for all time.

Every time we pray the Lord's prayer we say, "thy will be done." We ask for God's will to be done, but then we often fight it and flee from it. We want to control our lives. This is natural, especially in such a competitive society. Yet, what does Jesus ask of us? His agony before the passion tells us that we are off the track. We must right our direction in order to reach our promised inheritance of everlasting life.

Five minutes of prayer at the outset of each day can greatly aid us to achieve God's will in our lives. A simple meditation on Jesus' agony in Gethsemane and its meaning for us today works wonders. A slight modification of the Jesus Prayer repeated at the end of the meditation can benefit us. "Lord, Jesus, thy will be done." Beginning every day like this will reap a bountiful harvest and lead us to peace of mind.

We cannot control our lives totally, but we still try. The next time that things don't go as we think they should, reflect for a moment that God's will is being brought to reality. Let God be the pilot. The ride will bring us to unknown places and circumstances and bring fulfillment to our lives.

The Christian Call to Holiness

Our vocations in life are certainly varied. Some of us serve as teachers, social workers or doctors. Others work to help humanity through engineering, farming or science. Whatever our work, Christians all have one common vocation: the call to holiness. But a problem can arise if our personal desires for achievement overshadow our true vocation from God.

Isaiah 62:3-4 can bring back some reality to

our misguided desires. "You shall be a crown of beauty in the hand of the Lord, and a royal diadem in the hand of your God.... You shall be called my delight." Originally directed toward the Jews who had returned from exile, this passage speaks clearly to us today as well. God loves us for ourselves and what we are today, not for what we did yesterday or will do tomorrow. God loves us despite our failings, our brokenness and our sinfulness. We don't have to earn God's love, for the Lord delights in us already.

We live out our lives, sinful though they be, often without realizing that God loves us and asks us to impart that love to others. The vocation to holiness does not belong only to those actively engaged in professional ministry. It belongs to all the followers of Jesus, whether we desire it or not. Christ sent the apostles to evangelize the peoples of the world. We too have the task of bringing Jesus to all we meet. This can be done in many overt ways. But, even more today, Christ can be brought to colleagues, friends or people on the street by simple common gestures. A warm smile, an honest thank you, or a thoughtful gesture can bring Christ to another.

When we look at our lives it may dishearten us to see how much we have offended God. Yet as Isaiah says to us, God loves us today. He delights in us. If we remember this and try to center ourselves in his presence and love, then our vocation to holiness becomes a way of being rather than an isolated act of kindness. Despite our past faults and failings, God's love today can fire us with holiness.

As Christians we are called to make Christ real for others. St. Paul has urged us, "For as many of you as were baptized into Christ have put on Christ. There is neither Jew nor Greek, there is neither slave nor freeman, there is neither male nor female; for you are all one in Christ Jesus" (Gal 3:27-28). To put on Christ is not difficult. Jesus himself has told us, "My yoke is easy and my burden is light" (Mt 11:30). Once we have put on Christ we have found our vocation to holiness, a call to bring Christ to others in our daily lives.

Repentance

The need for repentance leaps out at me more and more each day. I have always realized that I am a sinner, yet I have only recently discovered the need for reconciliation with Jesus on a continuous basis.

Each day we labor through the brokenness in our lives. Hopefully our daily experiences teach us more about ourselves and our fellow men and women. But at times the lack of wholeness in each of us impairs our ability to see Jesus in others and stunts our growth in his presence. Why does our brokenness hinder our growth? This frustrating question overshadows the human dilemma described by philosophers and theologians from ancient times to the present.

Jesus gives us the solution to our brokenness. He is the way out of the dark pit which prevents us from seeing the light. As he himself stated, "I came not to call the righteous, but sinners" (Mk 2:17b). Jesus saves sinners. He is the solution to the brokenness we see in ourselves. Jesus offers us repentance. In Jesus, we always have a friend who stays with us and never forsakes us. He is the friend to whom we can cry out for repentance. He will heal our brokenness.

Jesus, our brother, came to show sinners the way to holiness. All we need to do is to open ourselves to the Spirit and allow him to direct and guide our actions. We hide in the shelter of the finite, but the Spirit of God can penetrate even the facade we throw up around ourselves. As Christians we are called to a life of holiness in Jesus Christ. We must be open to God's Spirit present in the world. Openness to the Spirit will lead us to repent, so that we can find comfort in the bosom of the Father.

Relaxing in the Lord

Many of us it find it difficult to relax in the presence of the Lord. So many urgent tasks crowd our busy schedules that it is difficult to spend time with the Lord. Yet, the hustle and bustle of our modern society makes it all the more necessary to find time to relax with God. Jesus even exhorts us to do this, "Come away by yourselves to a lonely place and rest a while" (Mk 6:31a).

Placing oneself in the presence of the Lord is the first step to feeling comfortable with God. Few of us have the advantage of structured retreat time in our schedules. But if we search, most of us can find twelve hours or possibly a full day to be alone with God. The process depends on exterior quiet to calm the soul. Being present to God is merely a state of peaceful quiet coupled with an openness of heart to let the Spirit take us where he wills. You will be amazed at where you will travel without even leaving your room!

Sacred Scripture furnishes us with an excellent means for spending time relaxing with the Lord. Reflecting on one or more short passages can provide the environment necessary to drift off with the Lord. We may use a reflection or meditation from the

Hebrew Scriptures, an event in the life of Jesus or a thought from the writings of St. Paul. Whatever we choose can lead us into that special tranquillity which we desire. A prayerful reading of the passage in a quiet atmosphere makes us open to the movement of the Spirit.

Sometimes we may find it difficult to concentrate, and so distractions creep in. This often occurs, but do not become discouraged. Offer your frustration and inattention to the Lord. Tell God you find it difficult to relax with him. You might be surprised at the subtle way in which the Lord will touch your heart in calling you back. All we need to bring to prayer is an openness to God and to the mysterious ways in which he works. God will provide whatever else is necessary for our time together in communion.

Although society often dictates the pace of our life, we need to slow down periodically and spend special time with God. Making this a regular routine in one's life can bring much peace and harmony in a fast paced existence. Although relaxing with the Lord requires a conscious effort, the resultant harvest brings a tranquillity that only God can give.

Have I Loved Today?

After a hard day at the office it is relaxing to sink into a comfortable chair, slip off one's shoes and take a break from the rush of the world. We probably consider our day a success if we finished our assigned tasks and kept the boss happy. That certainly counts for something, but we may be measuring our success by the world's standards, not by God's. To see how our day might look to God, we must ponder the question, "How much have I loved today?"

The Scriptures abound in references to love. But for me the fifteenth chapter of John epitomizes Jesus' teaching on the subject with the clear mandate, "This is my commandment, that you love one another as I have loved you" (Jn 15:12). We can do nothing greater than to show love to all the people we meet in our daily lives. It may seem difficult to show love to all, but Jesus presents us with this great challenge. It was no easier for the Christians of apostolic times who struggled with the conflict between law and freedom. St. Paul guided them when he wrote, "Love does no wrong to a neighbor; therefore love is the fulfilling of the law" (Rom 13:10).

How do we measure our progress? We could

answer this question in terms of economic status, position, productivity and personal achievement. Although many of these things have value, they do not show how much we have loved, which is all that God looks at. Our daily relationships with people should be guided by the spirit of John's Gospel. All our actions must point toward those elements which produce harmony. This high ideal challenges us, but also brings its own rewards. When we review our day we must see how we have carried the message of Christ to others. This does not necessarily mean quoting Scripture passages, but rather giving a lesson in the ethics and practices that Jesus taught. Today the laws of society and economics govern our daily actions. Yet we are Christians before we are business people. A Christian work ethic must guide us. Any other measure causes a conflict of interest for true followers of Christ.

Our contemporary society makes us aware of the many laws and statutes under which we live. Most people strive to uphold them. But we often forget the one law that matters, which is the ethic of Jesus with its command to love. We measure on the human scale but God sees things on a different plane. We may have to go out of our way to manifest God's love to others, but that is the one task that counts.

When you next evaluate your day try to see how much you have loved. Your score card in love will not reap monetary benefits in this life, but it will certainly please God. You will receive the elusive inner peace of mind and heart which alone can bring happiness and joy in this world and everlasting life in the world to come.

Whom Do I Love?

Contemporary society fires so much data at us that we can hardly sort it out. Television, radio, newspapers and magazines bombard us daily. We hear from friends, family and business associates. Many things, ideas and people vie for our attention and our love.

In such a fast-paced world we might ask, "Whom do I love?" It seems like a simple question with equally simple answers. We say, "I love my spouse and children," or "I love my parents." But these simple answers don't penetrate to the heart of the matter.

Exodus (32:1-34) recounts the idolatry of the Israelites, who made and worshipped a golden calf in violation of God's first commandment. This can appall us as we read about it. We easily pass judgment on ancient peoples. Yet, in many ways, those of us who live in the twentieth century lead lives of greater idolatry, although we may not recognize it.

What do I love? For some the honest answer may be power. We seek position and we hope that it will get us where we want to go. The ability to control and to dominate others can become a god. Some people love wealth. We may seek to amass more and more money and other worldly goods. People take notice if we drive a BMW or live on an estate. Others seek prestige. We may crave fame and recognition, as if that will make us happy.

Twentieth century idolaters are not bad people. They are you and I. The temptations of power, wealth and prestige surround us. But we must focus on the one who brings us joy and, eventually, eternal life—God. Many things can become gods for us, if we allow them to take over our lives. These gods tempt us because they exalt what our society values. But eventually, we find that their shallowness disappoints us and leaves us empty.

Living in God's presence gives our lives real purpose. When we keep our priorities straight and place God ahead of all, then worldly goods can help us attain God. They will not become the central point of our lives. Let us continue to focus on the Lord, who deserves our total love.

Love Yourself

An old Christian hymn says, "They will know we are Christians by our love, by our love. Yes, they'll know we are Christians by our love." Showing love to one another is one of the most basic teachings of Jesus. As the Lord says, "You shall love your neighbor as yourself" (Mk 12:31). It seems simple. All we need to do is to show we care, to help others and do works of service. This is possible for all and most of us do a satisfactory job. But we often brush over and even forget the basic premise that we need to love ourselves before we can begin to love others.

True self-love often eludes us, since low self-esteem troubles many of us. Our society constantly reinforces such negatives images. We must be tall enough, attractive enough and thin enough in order to succeed. We must have gone to the right school and know the proper people in order to get ahead. All of this pressure to measure up makes it difficult for us to feel good about ourselves. We may feel that we don't fit in. Our self-image is beaten down and sometimes even destroyed.

But our society misjudges success. All people are good because they are created in the image and likeness of God. Goodness does not necessarily translate into beauty, thinness, intelligence or personality. Rather, the principles of the Gospel determine goodness: service, humility, love of God and others. If we love God and work in his service and the service of all, then we display goodness. Such attitudes show our inherent dignity as humans. With such knowledge we can feel good about who we are. We can begin to love ourselves.

Once we love ourselves we can begin to love others. Without love our service and ministry remain empty. We need to love others and help them. But this can only be done with the joy and love of God which comes to us in faith.

Let us realize our special worth. As the popular car bumper sticker says, "God doesn't make junk." We are not junk but precious persons. We are loveable, by others and by ourselves. Let us love others so we too can carry out Jesus' command to love one another (cf. Jn 15:17).

From Darkness to Light

The early morning glows with its own special beauty. Darkness shadows the world, and stillness and calm dominate the scene. Looking to the east one glimpses a tinge of gold as it brushes the sky, a ray of hope that light will return. Dawn breaks as the sun rises slowly. At first the light illumines only the horizon. It then climbs higher in the eastern sky until the sun's rays penetrate the earth. Light dispels darkness and the bustle of the day displaces the hush of night.

As the sun turns night into day, so too does Jesus transform the darkness of our lives in the light of his presence. The problematic and sinful world in which we live shrouds all of us in darkness. Sin has filled the world with anxiety and doubt, pain and worry. We struggle with our human condition, a basic good which is constantly challenged by a world and society gone mad. Jesus cures sin and despair. He is the Lamb of God who takes away the sin and the darkness of the world. We need only allow Jesus to operate in our lives in order to find the solution to our world situation.

Jesus has told us, "I am the light of the world; he who follows me will not walk in darkness, but will have the light of life" (Jn 8:12). Jesus, the light, came to dispel the fear, ignorance and doubt which the darkness brings. Before Jesus, darkness shrouded the world. Now his light guides us. Sin has been defeated by the light of the world. Matthew tells us that people do not put a lamp under a bushel basket, but on a stand (5:15). Jesus, the light, cannot be effective in our lives if we hide him in a closet or close him away. If Jesus is allowed to shine forth, then, we, too, will shine brightly since we possess the light of life.

As the light of the world, Jesus came to live among us and to die for us. In the process he dispelled darkness and sin and conquered death. Sin and death no longer have a strangle-hold on humanity. Because of Jesus' redeeming action we live in the light and we can possess eternal life. All we need to do is to invite Jesus into our lives and let him shine even more brightly than the sun.

With Jesus on our side we can overcome the doubts and difficulties of this world. Jesus has given us all that we need to live and prosper as Christians. Let us dispel the darkness that sometimes creeps in. Let us walk with Jesus and turn darkness into light.

The Cross—Our Only Hope

"If any man would come after me, let him deny himself and take up his cross and follow me" (Mt 16:24). Jesus' great challenge to the disciples confronts us as well. If we want to go to Jesus, there is only one way—the cross. The cross of Jesus must be our only hope.

Spes unica—the cross our only hope—powerfully expresses and symbolizes our Christian witness in the world. How can an instrument of torture become a means of hope and open the way of salvation? The answer is simple but difficult to understand. God incarnate, Jesus the Christ, won victory for us and eternal life through his death on the cross. Through Jesus' death we have hope. The cross opens our way to the Lord.

It certainly seems contradictory to say that the cross is our hope. St. Paul put it well, "For the word of the cross is folly to those who are perishing, but to us who are being saved it is the power of God" (1 Cor 1:18). The cross leads us to God and gives us the means of gaining salvation with the Lord.

Denying oneself involves the cross. In a society which values achievement, position and personal growth, it requires heroism to deny oneself. It is counter-cultural and nonproductive in terms of society's standards. Self-denial need not harm us. Rather, such discipline imparts great strength to us personally and communally. Paul wrote that the runner in the race denies himself many things to win a crown of leaves which withers. But we deny ourselves to win a crown that lasts forever (cf. 1 Cor 9:25). Therefore, run so as to win the laurel that comes from God.

The most popular and easily recognized symbol of Christianity is the cross. We wear the cross to remind us of the paschal mystery of the passion, death and resurrection of the Lord. But we wear and display the cross in order to bring hope as well. It gives hope to a world in which crime, violence and abuse choke out life. It gives hope to a world in which sin and brokenness shatter human lives. Let the cross stand out as our sign. It is our principal sign of hope. Let the cross and our self-denial bring us closer to God.

Follow Me

All of us admire heroes and heroines, those people whom we respect and look up to. Their lives inspire us so powerfully that we want to follow in their footsteps. As children, we often idolize sports figures, movie and television stars or popular musicians. As we get older, our heroes change to politicians, civil organizers or religious leaders. Names such as Dorothy Day, Mother Teresa of Calcutta or Maximilian Kolbe stand out as such heroes.

Heroes inspire us to imitate them. We wish to take their beliefs and actions and make them our own. We hope to become better people by modeling our lives on theirs.

In many ways Jesus was a hero to Peter. Jesus chose Peter as the leader of the apostles. Although Peter never seemed to get things right and lapsed in faith, Jesus chose him to be the apostle to the Jews. Peter was pragmatic and down to earth. He doesn't seem to have been a person of vision or a dreamer. Nevertheless, through the wonder of God, Peter was attracted to Jesus, dropped everything and became an apostle.

As Jesus' time on earth drew to a close he told his friend Peter, "Follow me" (Jn 21:19b). Since Jesus was Peter's hero, he was probably happy to do just that: follow the Lord. But I am certain that Peter had no idea what that simple command would entail. Jesus went on to tell Peter how others would bind him and carry him off against his will. That was part of the "follow me." In the beginning, Peter never thought that following the Lord would lead him to death.

Jesus' command to Peter is his command to us as well. Although we may admire other people as our heroes in the short run, God must be our hero in the end. As the incarnate Word of God, Jesus has given us an example of life and love which he asks us to imitate. Living such a life means dying to self so that others may prosper. Following Jesus involves a lifetime commitment to service, imitating the servant of all.

Jesus simply says, "Follow me." But how difficult that can be. So many things and people demand our loyalty. Our work, our leisure and the heroes of our life ask us to follow them. Let us keep our priorities straight and follow the Lord. This journey leads ultimately to death, but death ushers us into eternal life with God.

Thank You, God

If you look to the west, you can see it every night, usually glowing gold and red. Sometimes clouds or buildings obscure its view. Its time of appearance changes during the year. Sunset treats us to a magnificent sight. With the dusk, God whispers good night to the world.

Genesis tells us that God created the sun to rule the day and the moon to govern the night. Like our God, the sun provides the light which dominates our day. Try to imagine a world without the sun. It would not only be dark, but cold and unwelcoming as well. God provides the light to live and work. The darkness provides a time for rest so that once again we can greet the day, refreshed and renewed.

After the sun has run its course each day, it begins to set. It's as if God says good night to the world he created. God certainly never abandons us, and the sunset gently reminds us that God has been with us this day. As God bids us rest to renew our energies for the next day, so too must we bid good night to God.

Prayer is an excellent way to bid good night to God. Most of us excel at prayer of petition. When we need something, we go to God, who will certainly listen to and answer our requests. The lines of communication between God and humanity are always open. But I wonder how often we turn to prayer of thanksgiving. When we wake up in the morning do we take time to thank God? When we arrive safely at work after perhaps risking our lives on the highway do we thank God? When we have sufficient food for the day do we take a moment to pray in gratitude to God? When we go to bed do we say thank you to God for the day, just for living, knowing that many people will not see or enjoy tomorrow?

Our prayer of good night cannot match the

beauty and power of the sunset, but that's not important. What matters is to remain in communication with God. Saying thank you, good morning or good night to God keeps us connected to him. God communicates with us through the beauty of nature, through Scripture and through people. Let us speak with our God in prayer and thank God for each day.

Re-Creation

The sun peeks over the eastern horizon. Its rays bathe the earth with warmth as the animals awake and creep out of their burrows. The world begins to rouse from its slumber. Dawn breaks.

Each day's dawn brings a newness to our world, as if the world is beginning all over again. After the night has spent itself, the day draws near. The work of God's creation again becomes visible and the human race is guided on its way. The newness breathes a freshness which smells clean and appears in a new beauty. Each dawn gifts us with a re-creation of God's love and presence in our world.

Genesis tells us that God created the world in six days. But God did not stop creating after his initial work. No, God continually re-creates our world, day by day. God even re-creates us.

The dynamic forces of our world continually sculpt and refashion God's original work. Volcanoes erupt and new islands form in the sea, or the terrain changes beyond recognition. Earthquakes rumble through the earth as its tectonic plates shift and slide into new positions. The land takes on new shapes. Storms erode beaches and rivers gouge new routes through canyons and valleys. The earth is constantly being re-created.

As the dawn heralds God's daily re-creation of our environment, so humans are re-created as well. Our re-creation begins with baptism which makes us members of God's family. The water purifies us and gives us a new beginning in Christ. Baptism as a sacrament occurs only once. Yet we need to celebrate and live each day the re-creation which baptism gives. Jesus redeemed us for all time by his painful death on the cross. Each time we think of Jesus and his life and actions for us, we have the opportunity of being re-created. Each time Jesus comes to us in prayer, reflection, Scripture and in others, he brings us the opportunity to grow, to be changed and to be re-created by God.

Just as the dawn always comes, endless opportunities for re-creation await us. Each day the dawn beckons us to begin anew in our quest to find God and to cast off the darkness which sometimes pervades our life. God is in all; God is everywhere. But if we fail to grasp the opportunities that God presents to us, then we miss an opportunity for growth, recreation and the chance to see God himself. Let the dawn encourage us to seek renewal. Let Jesus recreate us this day!

God Waters the Earth

The rains flowed down from the heavens. At times they pounded the earth and at other times they gently showered the ground. Parched from drought, the earth lapped up the water like a thirsty deer. Some of the water ran off, but most soaked into the ground, nourishing and replenishing the soil.

Before long, the earth began to yield fruit from the waters of heaven. Streams began to flow again through the countryside. Seeds long dormant began to sprout, bringing beauty to the fields. Flowers bloomed and the grass turned green once more. Even the birds played in the pools that the rain formed. Chipmunks drank from the streams again.

The rains that flow from heaven, nurturing and beautifying, are like our God who waters our earth. God waters our earth each day. God nurtures us not only in the gentle rains which give drink to the land, but in the many ways in which he feeds us. God bathes our world in sunlight, giving warmth to our hearts and nourishment to our bodies. God nurtures us in darkness, calming the speed and anxiety of the day and cooling the sun's mighty rays. God showers us with grace, his special gift. It can come through an insight at work or school. It can come through God's revelation in Scripture, prayer or liturgical celebrations. God's grace can come through those around us, through their smile, their warm welcome or their gentle embrace. God waters our earth each day. We only need to recognize it.

Rain pours down, but through the darkness and gloom of the day I know that God is smiling as he waters the earth. God nurtures the nature which surrounds us. God waters us as well, many times each day. Faith helps us recognize the hand of God as it sustains us each day. The skies may drop down snow or rain, the sun may burn oppressively hot, or the day may be beautiful. Whatever the weather, God waters the earth and provides for humanity at the same time. Let us find our strength and sustenance in the Lord this day. Let us be thankful that God has watered our earth.

Who Do You Say I Am?

"Who do you say that I am?" (Mt 16:15). The Lord asked Peter such a simple question. Jesus had chosen Peter as one of the twelve. Peter had walked with the Lord. He had listened to Jesus' preaching and teaching. Peter had dropped everything to follow Jesus. Yet, our Lord still asked Peter, "Who do you say that I am?" Peter's answer demonstrated his faith. "You are the Christ, the Son of the living God." Jesus congratulated Peter on his insight, saying that Peter's knowledge came not from human sources, but from God.

To us as well, Jesus directs the question that he asked Peter. To each person Jesus says, "Who do you say that I am?" We can give the quick answer that we have heard so many times: Jesus is Lord. We can say without thought that Jesus is our friend. But do we believe it? Will others know that we are friends of Jesus by what they hear and observe in us? "Who do you say that I am?" poses a powerful and difficult question for our modern society. Many people and ideas vie for our attention. Society makes so many demands on our busy lives that we tend to relegate Jesus to second place. If this is true, then in honesty we cannot profess the faith of Peter.

Who is Jesus for us? Our answers will vary but they should not surprise us. For some, Jesus is the hour we spend at church on Sunday. For some, Jesus is an obligation. We may fear what the good sister said in grade school or CCD and we march off to church, however reluctantly. Our attitude bespeaks that children need Jesus, but not adults. We may think that we've grown out of the need. Jesus has become a habit. He is someone who lingers, but our need for God has slipped away. For some Jesus is a statue, a half-hearted "Our Father" or a well-thumbed prayer book. But Jesus must be more for those who profess to be Christians.

Jesus the Christ, the anointed of God, must take first place in our lives. Jesus must open the gateway to service. Jesus must bring us into the life of joy and happiness which only God can give. Jesus lives in our hearts and should be manifest to all by how we lead our lives. Jesus is the source of eternal life for all. We should delight in the pleasure of professing our belief in him.

"Who do you say that I am?" This simple question challenges us to answer truthfully. Let Jesus be for us, as for St. Peter, the Christ, the anointed one, the one who redeems us and our world.

The Journey to God

Life is a journey. While we live in this world we are constantly on the move. It may be a physical move as we travel to a new geographic area. It may be a career move or simply a shift in attitude.

As we constantly move, we might ask ourselves where we are going. Where will our move take us? We may move to another city or state or even out of the country. We may shift our position at work or change careers. We may be moving in our political beliefs or social interests. Hopefully, all of our moves take us further along our journey to God.

The journey to God entails a lifetime project. Each opportunity to answer the call to change invites us to journey to God. Change makes us re-evaluate our lives. Change forces us to slow down or even to stop. Such moments in our hectic lives give God the best opportunity to work. Unfortunately, our fast-paced society tends to eliminate God and relegates the Creator to second place.

The journey to God challenges us, but nothing worthwhile in life comes without effort. The journey to God is lived out in the day-to-day struggles of our lives. When we encounter some situation, event or person that asks us to move from our present position, then we have also discovered a path to God. When we consider life changes, we find ways that God challenges us to move and to refine our attitudes and beliefs toward God and other people.

The goal of our life is to return to God, the one from whom we came. Ecstasy and tragedy befall us along the return trip. At times it may seem that we will never reach our goal. Yet, if we allow ourselves to grow and be changed by God, the return trip is not only more possible, but more pleasant. Each day life challenges us to continue our journey to God.

Let us continue our journey despite difficulties and changes, which will inevitably come. We needn't fight these changes. As the metaphor of the potter in the prophet Jeremiah suggests, we can allow life's changes to remold us into the image of God, the one who came to bring us home (cf. Jer 18:1-10).

Our Relationship with God

Society constantly evaluates its members. It begins from our earliest days in school. We strive to attain good grades, since our teachers and counselors gauge our academic performance. They accordingly peg us as excellent, average or failing students. Our citizenship and deportment are also evaluated. People want to know how well we perform at sports. We're scored on how fast we run or swim, and how far we hit the ball. In business we face job reviews for promotion, greater responsibility or a higher salary. We have to constantly prepare for all of these evaluations. We try to do our best in school, work feverishly in our jobs or impress the community with our devotion. All of this marks our way of life today.

But are we equally concerned about our relationship with God? Are we concerned about the one evaluation which really matters? As St. Paul wrote to the Christian community at Rome, "Each of us shall give account of himself to God. Then let us no more pass judgment on one another, but rather decide never to put a stumbling block or hindrance in the way of a brother" (Rom 4:12-13). The only appraisal which counts is the one given us by our God. It produces no marketable rewards in this life, but achieves our life's goal, which is union with God.

If we are doing well in God's sight, then the seemingly important evaluations of this life will fall into perspective. If we are right with God then we are right with ourselves. This internal feeling of peace gives us the means to succeed in our world. If we don't feel good about ourselves, then we will have great difficulty convincing others of our worth, whether in regard to academics, sports or business.

Assessments play an important part in this life, and for eternal life as well. We may shrink with fear at the thought of giving an account of our actions before God. But if we live in God's presence, if we live for others and not for ourselves, imitating the service of Jesus, then God will give us a positive rating. God does not ask us to be perfect, but only that we constantly strive to do better. Let us strive to do our best in everything. But most especially, let us dedicate ourselves to the service of others, spending our lives for God's people. If we do this then all our evaluations will lead to our final goal, which is peace in the palm of God's hand.

The Reward

We give and receive presents for various occasions. The giving of gifts marks such special events as birthdays, anniversaries and Christmas. Presents also show up for such major accomplishments as graduation, promotion or some victory. We often give gifts because we have done something. We've reached a milestone or cleared a hurdle and we celebrate that event. Other times, presents are given merely through the generosity of the giver, who gives out of love, without recompense.

God has given humanity so many gifts that we can't comprehend them all. We have our world, our lives and our faith. We have Jesus, God incarnate, who came to die so that we might have life. Even more wonderfully, God continues to shower us with gifts, not for what we have done or will do, but merely out of love. He asks nothing in return except our love. All the gifts awaiting us will surely be magnificent. St. Paul wrote, "No eye has seen, nor ear heard, nor the heart of man conceived what God has prepared for those who love him" (1 Cor 2:9). We do not deserve such gifts. Yet God will bestow such marvels on us that we can never grasp or comprehend their magnificence.

Most of us wonder, "What will heaven be like?" As finite beings looking to an infinite God, we can only speculate and dream. But one thing is certain. God's eternal reward for those who love him will surpass our highest expectations. With all the wonders on earth that the eye can see and all the beauty that the ear can hear, we can only marvel that God has prepared such a magnificent place for us.

God does not ask much. Jesus gave us the two great commandments, which are to love God above all things and to love our neighbor as ourself. Love does not injure others but fulfills the law. God asks us to love. It might not be possible to like all people and associate with them. The world is too big and complex for that. But God asks us to love and respect all, no matter who they are or where they may be. In showing love for others we show love for our Creator. In this way, we fulfill the law in imitation of the example Jesus gave us in the Gospels.

Gifts come in all shapes and sizes, wrapped in bright paper and decorated with ribbons. Presents come for what we have done, and they also come for no other reason than love. "God so loved the world that he gave his only Son, that whoever believes in him should not perish but have eternal life" (Jn 3:16). God sent us Jesus, who opened the way for us to an eternal life beyond our grasp. Let us accept God's magnificent generosity and seek to show love in return.

The Cross

When I was a little boy I always carried a cross in my pocket. Actually, it wasn't a cross at all, but a circular flat piece of wood which had the cross etched into it. I can't remember if my parents gave it to me or if I received it at church. But I know that I carried it wherever I went. It reminded me of Jesus and what he did for us.

As an adult I still treasure the cross. I don't carry it in my pocket, but wear it around my neck. I bought it many years ago when I was in the navy. It's small, flat and silver. It's a small sign, but it serves a big purpose in reminding me of what the cross means.

The cross symbolizes my faith. It not only means that I am Christian, but it reminds me of the events of Jesus' life and what his supreme sacrifice gave me and all humanity. Through the cross we find life today and eternal salvation with God as well. Jesus said yes to his Father through the cross. For us, each day the cross can be a way of saying thank you to Jesus for what he continually does for us.

As a symbol, the cross need not only be something we keep in our pocket or wear around our neck. The cross should be indelibly etched into our soul. We can't see it there, but we can see how it affects our actions, both ours and those of others. If the cross has become part of us, then our lives will reflect the self-sacrifice and renunciation that the cross symbolizes. We begin to live more for others by sharing their pain and rejoicing in their triumphs.

The cross inspires us to put others first. We carry Jesus' cross when we strive to make our world a better place for all.

As a symbol of Jesus' redeeming action in our world, the cross sheds hope on the future. If we see the cross solely as an instrument of torture then we miss its true power. The cross must lead us to love and hope. Out of love, Jesus chose to die for us. We live in hope of our own resurrection, achieved through Jesus' death. Let us keep a cross in our pocket or around our neck. Let us live the action of the cross in our daily lives.

Discipleship

"Come follow me." That call of Jesus lured Peter and his brother Andrew. They dropped everything and followed the Lord. Jesus then caught James and John. They abandoned their father Zebedee in the boat and became Jesus' disciples.

In Scripture the call to discipleship seems so easy and complete. None of the apostles hesitated for a moment. Suddenly Jesus transformed their whole lives. They asked no questions but obediently did as the Lord bid them. The call of Jesus powerfully attracted them and perhaps even overwhelmed them.

The call to discipleship still comes to us today. But we often complicate our lives so that we can't hear the call. Most of us wish we could drop an activity or two to make our lives more sane. We look at discipleship as an added activity or even a burden that we just can't find time for in our busy schedule.

Jesus calls us just as he called the apostles. Today we look at discipleship as an activity. Rather, we should see it as a way of life. Certainly Peter and his comrades no longer worked as fishermen after they met Jesus. They walked in his footsteps and listened to his words. But this radically altered their perspective and their understanding of life. Raised in the Jewish tradition, the apostles realized that Jesus had radicalized the teachings of ancient Israel. They had to change their thinking to accept Jesus as Lord. Similarly, we must look at discipleship as a way of life for us. We need not change jobs, lifestyle or location. But we do need to change our understanding and priorities to truly follow in the footsteps of the Lord. Our renewed understanding must place Jesus as our first priority and relegate everything else to second place.

Discipleship demands a lifetime commitment. Discipleship may even demand our life itself. In *The Cost of Discipleship*, the famous Lutheran pastor and theologian Dietrich Bonhoeffer says that following the Lord will eventually require one's life. Eternal life does not cost money, but the road of discipleship leading to salvation costs us everything. This should not surprise us. Millions have marched the road before us and spent themselves for the Lord, whether in large or small measure. Being disciples of the Lord enriches our lives. Thus, giving our lives to God in the service of others should fulfill us.

The Lord Jesus calls us. His call comes in the profound moments of life as well as in the mundane. His "Come follow me" invites us to holiness and eternal life. Let us respond to the call and renew our commitment as his disciples today.

Understanding

How many times have we heard or said, "I just wish they understood me." Young people moan this about their parents. Employees say it about supervisors. Students say it about their teachers. To understand others challenges us. It requires us to go out of ourselves. We must look through the eyes of another, with that person's perspective and background in order to understand. Many shy away from the difficulty. Rather, we often think that people should see things from our perspective. Thus, understanding becomes a precious commodity in our world.

Jesus understood others better than anyone. As finite human beings, we can't fathom or understand God. But there is no need, for God understands us. God knows us thoroughly, and even stooped down to enter our world. God became a human being in Jesus Christ our Lord. As the beautiful hymn in Philippians states, "Though he was in the form of God, [he] did not deem equality with God a thing to be grasped, but emptied himself, taking the form of a servant, being born in the likeness of men" (Phil 2:6-7). Jesus became a man to live among us, to understand us better. He was born of human estate so that God could be united to the human race. Whether we realize it or not, God understands us better than anyone. God chose to become human and to experience the human state.

Like many things in life, understanding goes in two directions. We want others to understand us, and others ask us to understand them. If we wish to understand others, then we must be willing to try to enter their world. Hospital training tells us that we can never fully understand another, because we are not that person. But if we choose, we can relate and try to see things from another's eyes. Only then can we begin to have the compassion and patience needed for understanding.

If we feel frustrated when others don't understand us, we still have a place to go. Go to the Lord in prayer. Jesus can and does understand us. Jesus accepts us with infinite compassion and patience. Jesus does not speak to us as other people do. But in the silence of prayer and the events of life, our Lord answers us better than any loving parent or friend.

Understanding requires something of us. We must listen and be present. We must take the time to enter another's world. Let us try to understand others better, imitating Jesus, the one who became human so as to experience the reality of human life.

Abandonment

Have you ever felt abandoned? Have you ever felt that nobody cared? Have your friends deserted you, especially when you needed them most? Abandonment can desolate us. It causes an emptiness which we can never adequately describe. When we are abandoned we have no one to whom we can go and are utterly alone.

Jesus tasted that feeling of abandonment more than most. The events leading to his crucifixion show us a classic case of abandonment. At the Last Supper, Judas left first. Judas had lost his incentive to follow Jesus. The magnetism had evaporated, along with Judas' loyalty to the Lord. Peter and the sons of Zebedee, James and John, deserted Jesus next. Jesus took them with him into the Garden of Gethsemane that same night. Jesus prayed fervently, "My Father, if it be possible, let this cup pass from me; nevertheless, not as I will, but as you will" (Mt 26:39b). Jesus later returned and found his comrades asleep, "So, could you not watch with me one hour?" (Mt 26:40b). Twice more Jesus found his disciples asleep after his return from prayer. Later Peter denied Jesus three times, as the Lord had predicted. At Calvary, the Gospels tell us that John was the only apostle who stood by the cross. Where were the other ten? In his most needy moment, Jesus' best friends had forsaken him.

Lest we think that only the apostles have abandoned the Lord, let us look at our own lives. When we refuse the Lord's daily invitations to holiness and faith, when we abandon our brothers and sisters in need, then most certainly we have deserted the Lord. Jesus seems to be regularly rejected and abandoned these days. In certain ways the agony in the garden still continues for Jesus. As Pascal so beautifully put it, "Christ will be in agony until the end of the world. During that time, we must not sleep!"

Although we may have often abandoned the Lord, his loving mercy still surrounds us. Jesus' resurrection conquered death forever. It also showed how the abandoned can still triumph. Jesus was abandoned by all, except his Father. We too can rejoice to think that God will never leave us.

Sometimes we experience abandonment ourselves. When we need them the most, our friends, colleagues and loved ones may refuse to support us. That sinking feeling fills us and we do not know where to turn. But we can turn to the Lord. Not only does he know the agony of abandonment, but Jesus has told us that he will be with us until the end of the world. When abandonment strikes, we won't find the solution in outside activities or old friends from the past. We'll find the solution in the Lord. If we feel abandoned or lonely, let us find consolation, solace and companionship in Jesus, the one who was abandoned, the one who is brother, friend and Lord to us all.

Never Alone

The plane streaks through the sky at 600 miles per hour, at an altitude of 33,000 feet. I feel alone, but I know that I am not alone. After a great time with my best friend who is driving somewhere on the road below, I'm going home. Although we must part, we are never truly separated.

The complicated and complex world in which we live often forces friends and family to part. Business takes us across the country and sometimes over the oceans. People travel thousands of miles and hardly think about it. The distance and the amount that we travel would have amazed our grandparents.

When we travel we leave others behind. Such separations are common, but that does not make them any easier. When I leave people behind, I know that I am not alone. God stays with me, always at my side, walking with me along the road of life. God's presence goes beyond being a substitute or consolation for the one we miss. God is the reason for life. God gives us what we need. If we have not left God behind, then we should never be lonely.

Unfortunately for many, God is the first person left behind. Career, family and recreation rob God of the first place in our lives. It cannot be that way if we profess to be Christians. Through baptism our lives become God centered. Baptism stamped us with an indelible mark on our souls, the mark of God's presence, the mark of our commitment to God.

We often feel lonely, whether we're flying across the country, driving through the desert or rocking in an easy chair at home. When loneliness strikes, when that sick feeling of emptiness invades our being, there is only one way to turn. Give the loneliness and emptiness to God. God can fill the void and allow us to feel whole again. The important people of our life, those for whom we long, become closer when we think of them as God's messengers to us, even if they are physically distant. They bring God to us through their presence, word and actions.

Separations cause sorrow. But when we believe with full certainty that our friends and family bring God to us, then we are never alone. Let God be our partner. Let us walk with the Lord and never be lonely again.

What Is Peace?

What is peace? How can we define it? *Webster's Dictionary* states that peace is a state of tranquillity; it is freedom from civil disturbance.

This definition may satisfy us, but it still falls short. This definition implies that peace is passive, that all we need to do is to eliminate strife and problems and peace will reign. On the contrary, peace demands an active commitment, and can only be attained by our positive efforts. Peace requires work.

Images of peace abound in Scripture, but for me the prophet Isaiah provides the most vivid imagery. He speaks of wolves lying down with lambs, and lions with calves. He paints a scene in which a baby will play at the cobra's den and no harm shall come to all God's holy mountain (cf. Is 11:1-10). These images seem so unlikely that we wonder how such a thing could ever happen. Such peace can only be achieved by active effort, not by passive negligence. If we want peace, we must be willing to pay the price by working to build a just society where people can live in harmony.

In order to build community, we must become peacemakers. Such a task daunts us and is fraught with obstacles. But the peacemaking process must begin with ourselves.

Reconciliation is the best way to start. We need to be reconciled to ourselves, to God and to God's people. Through the sacrament of Penance we can find the personal reconciliation we need in our journey toward being peacemakers. Through Penance we discover anew our reasons for life, and return to greater self respect. Best of all, we can renew our relationship with God.

Once we have been reconciled with ourselves and with God, then our peacemaking efforts must extend to our community, our Church, and ultimately to our world. If we want peace in our streets then we must do something to create an environment which promotes harmony among neighbors. If we want peace to reign in the minds of our children, then we must actively pursue peace in our lives and reflect it to others in what we say and do. If we want peace in our world, then governments, leaders and nations must be willing to extend a welcoming hand, showing how differences can be worked out around the conference table instead of a battlefield. If we want peace in our homes, we might need to sacrifice our personal needs for the good of all.

Pope Paul VI once stated, "If you want peace, work for justice." In seven words the Pope summed up the active message of peace. Peace follows in the wake of justice, but justice can only happen with active involvement by all, an involvement which promotes dignity and equality for all humanity. Let us work for peace and justice. Let us find harmony with one another in imitation of Jesus, the Prince of Peace.

Dare to Hope

Do you dare to hope? Are you optimistic? When we look at the world around us, it may seem difficult to find something positive. Drug abuse and the crime it breeds permeate our society. Violence frightens people into staying in at night, and to always seek a companion when traveling. Economic problems play havoc with the savings of those on fixed incomes, and throw people out of work. It's difficult to keep an optimistic outlook. Can the demise of hope lag far behind?

People today use the terms hope and optimism almost interchangeably. But hope differs from optimism. It may be true that we lack optimism, especially when we look at the world. But hope differs from optimism. Hope abounds in the hearts, desires and faith of many. Hope means that despite the problems, fear and uncertainty of the present, something good will result from today's pain and tragedy, and draw us closer to God.

I believe that if we honestly ponder it, we can see that good has come from what seemed so negative and bad. The death of a relative or close friend can shatter us. When we lose our job we don't know which way to turn. If some circumstance injures us or side-tracks us from our goals, we become angry. Although at the time these events cause great suffering and pain, they can bring growth and draw us closer to God. Even though they disrupt the calmness and direction of our life, we can see the hand of God guiding us. Events cause us to rethink and refocus. Difficult times tell us that we need to change. Maybe we depended too much on another, or perhaps we needed to slow down and gain a new perspective. It takes time, but generally we can find the silver lining to the most dense and foreboding cloud. This can give us a sense of hope, which helps us realize that something positive can result from the negative events of our life.

"Dare to hope" should be the Christian motto. The Christian can always hope. We can possess hope because eventually we can see the blessings of even the most tragic setbacks. We can also be filled with hope because we know that the Spirit of God abides with us. Our hope is strong and solid for we know that with God all things are possible. Daring to hope challenges the pessimism of the world with confidence in our God.

Despite the pain and insanity of our world, we have reasons for hope. Jesus came to save us, to lift us from our brokenness and inspire us to continue our daily journey. Let us dare to hope despite a world which gives little credence to our faith. Let us see the presence of God in all we do today.

Surrender Brings Peace

The unknown and uncertain often fill us us with apprehension and fear. We like to know where we are going and what we will be doing. We love to plan and figure out our lives down to the last second. When some event or person brings uncertainty, we panic and don't know what to do. A certain element of doubt has entered our life and we feel insecure.

Since we don't know the future, we can easily fear it. We instinctively fear what we do not know. Whether it is a new tool or machine, the computer system at work or an unfamiliar detour route, anxieties mount when we face the unknown. We react against it. We do whatever we can to remove the uncertainty and regain control of the situation. Sometimes we even go out of our way to assure that we can avoid the new tool, computer or route.

We can never totally banish from our lives

uncertainty and the apprehension it breeds. Things never go just as expected, since life is not that simple. The interruptions and uncertainties offer us opportunities to grow, learn and become more complete. Since we cannot prevent such disturbances and they can help us grow, the best solution to the problem may be to let things happen and not fight the inevitable.

Surrender to God is the best answer of all. The uncertainty can come from God. Maybe it is a way to slow us down or a way that God invites us to do something different. It can challenge us to move beyond the comfortable into more demanding avenues and facets of life. If we surrender to God, then the doubts and fears can help us make the kingdom more fully present now. If we allow God to guide us and if we rely less on our own wisdom, then we are surely walking safely along the right road. As the book of Proverbs says, "Trust in the Lord with all your heart, and do not rely on your own insight. In all your ways acknowledge him, and he will make straight your paths" (Prov 3:5-6). If we can let go of our need to control, then God will enter our lives and miracles can happen.

Uncertainty will often intrude on our lives. Rather than fighting it and becoming frustrated and angry, let us surrender our lives to God and allow him to do with us what pleases him, today and every day of our lives.

Generosity

The famous American poet John Greenleaf Whittier once wrote that kindness bestowed on others will return to the giver. The words of Whittier come back to me during festivities, whether they be birthdays, holidays or other family celebrations. I don't think that I have done anything special. I haven't felt that my presence has made a difference. If Whittier is correct, the kindness that I receive has returned to the place from which it came.

The kindness which others show to us flows from generosity. Generosity involves giving, but not only that. Generosity requires an attitude of kindness to others. It reflects mutual feelings of kindness and love.

Sometimes the kindness of others overwhelms us. They shower us with gifts and presents. People invite us to their homes to visit, share meals and renew friendships. At times it seems that generosity comes quite unexpectedly. We wonder why people can so generously share their time, skill and resources.

Kindness stems from generosity. But the root of generosity goes even deeper. Generosity is born from love, a love centered in the Lord which reaches out to all others. A person who doesn't love withers up. When one loves, then the world brightens. People begin to smile and generosity transforms us. Like love, generosity is not something that we can buy. Rather, generosity forms part of who we are. If we truly love others, then that love can never be destroyed. It takes root in our being. The people we love become us and we become them. Similarly, true generosity can never be separated from us. Generosity is who we are.

If we wish to be more generous to others, we must first learn to be people of greater love. We love others by loving God, the one who first loved us. Let us love God and in the process become more generous. The love, kindness and generosity which we display will return in ways which we can only imagine.

Come to Me

"Come to me, all who labor and are heavy laden, and I will give you rest" (Mt 11:28). Jesus invites us in this simple yet challenging way. We might think it obvious that when problems burden us and life wearies us, people would come to the Lord. It seems so easy, but in reality it's difficult. The world allures us as it seeks to assuage our problems with a drink at the bar or sordid entertainment. We look for solutions to life's problems apart from God. Jesus invites us to come to him. He does not ask us to run, since he realizes that obstacles stand in the way. He only asks us to come at our own pace, pick ourselves up when we fall, and continue our journey to the Lord.

The Lord bids us to come to him, but many times we find ourselves attracted to other people and things. The allurements of this world can capture our hearts. The world tells us over and over again that problems can be resolved instantly, without waiting or work. We can command instant cash, instant credit and instant pain relief. But we know that the instants of our world do not last long and soon fade away, like dew in the morning sun. The world cons us with the idea that we can get by with as little effort as possible. But in reality, instant solutions usually don't work for long. We can find the true solution to our daily problems only in God. God wants us to come to him to find solutions and help.

Many hurdles and obstacles crop up in our

lives. We can overcome some of them easily, while others require more effort. These obstacles cause us to change direction or shift gears. After overcoming such stumbling blocks, we can sense a difference in our lives. If we have managed to continue toward God, then the problems challenged us to grow. If we have failed to pick ourselves up from the blows life delivered, then those hurdles hindered us on our journey. When adversity strikes, Christians pick themselves up from the ground and continue toward the Lord. Jesus urges us, "Come to me." It doesn't matter if we run or crawl. All that matters is to keep going, to keep moving in our journey to God. All of us have come from God, and we desire to return to God.

Let us go to God today. Jesus invites us to join him. We can't refuse him. Let us move through the challenges which God gives us today, and in the process find the kingdom alive in our hearts.

Saying Goodbye

We hugged each other that last evening. She cried openly and I cried invisible tears of the heart. As we said goodbye, we felt the sorrow of parting. Loved ones and best friends find it difficult to leave each other. Our hearts desire the companionship of those whom we love. When we have to separate, it seems that a part of us leaves with the other person, leaving us incomplete.

As difficult as partings are, I can honestly admit that I never say goodbye. Goodbye has a note of finality. When one says goodbye, there may never be another meeting. When one says goodbye, the parting may be final.

When farewells come in our life, hopefully we can always say that we will see each other again. For people who have a special bond, the leave-taking is never permanent. Friends never fully separate because they are a part of each other. Close friends find it impossible to separate the feelings and emotions which bind them together. Best friends and people in love can never really say goodbye.

We can know that the ones we love are never far away when we look at our God. When Jesus left the earth he sent his Spirit to abide with us always. We cannot see, hear or touch the Spirit, but we can feel his presence with us. The manifestations of the Spirit fill the world, and we need only open our minds and hearts to recognize them. God is always near as the best of friends who never abandons us. We cannot cut God out from our being or escape his love. God stays with us every moment of every day, lighting and guarding the path which leads back to him.

Relationships with close friends resemble relationships with God. We can feel the presence of others, for even if they are physically distant, they are still close to our hearts. True friendships and love begin and grow in the mind, heart and soul. If a friendship permeates our heart and soul, then that friend remains present to us.

The next time that a parting occurs in your life, remember God's relationship with the human race and realize that you never need to say goodbye. God is always with us. So too are our special friends and loved ones. If we believe this, then we can be grateful for God's present and rejoice in our relationships, especially in our close friends.

Parents

Parents are amazing people. With the help of God they bring us into the world. During our childhood they play a critical role in our lives. They feed us and clothe us and provide us with a place to sleep. They shelter us from danger. They smile, hug us and come to our aid when we need them. Parents shower true love on us, as they sacrifice themselves for our good.

Parents give good example. They take care of everything, from showing us how to tie our shoes, to walking with us on that first day of school. Parents teach us the rudiments of the faith by word, but especially by example. Children learn to love from the way that their parents love them. Through their parents children learn to love themselves as well as each other. The way that parents approach life influences their children. Pensive parents who constantly worry teach their children to worry, too. If parents can place things in God's hands with trust, then so will their children.

Hopefully parents and children have good relationships. If they show mutual respect and love, then certainly harmony will reign in the family. This helps everyone grow. If parents and children fail to display a common love and respect, the results can devastate the family. The love which Jesus showed toward all during his earthly lifetime must be our model.

A parent's role never ends. Time shows us that parenting in the formative years paves the way for parenting in the adult years. Parents who love their children find different ways to express this affection as time passes. Teaching children about the basics of life translates into support in later life.

Parents give their children advice based on their own experience. When difficulties arise with work, spouse or children, parents will lend a hand. Parents never give up but continue to show their love and concern to the end.

I'm fortunate that my mother and father continue to be my parents. They love, support and respect me for who I am today. Over time, our relationship has continued to grow in wonderful and powerful ways. God has blessed me with wonderful parents. I hope that my respect for them is apparent. They have taught me what it means to be a person of faith; they have taught me how to love. May my love for them imitate the love God shows us today and each day of our lives.

Not One Shall Be Lost

At times it seems that God makes no sense. In a world which idolizes progress, accomplishment and majority rule, it doesn't make much sense to leave ninety-nine perfectly good and well-behaved sheep in order to search for one that is lost. A grade of ninety-nine percent fulfills the most rigorous standards and merits an "A." But ninety-nine percent doesn't satisfy God, because our God desires that none should be lost. Jesus the Good Shepherd never gives up on us. Like the hound of heaven in Francis Thompson's famous poem, God pursues us even if we dart through alleys and back roads. God will go to the highest mountain or the deepest valley in search of that one who has strayed. God will search in winter blizzards and summer's scorching heat. God desires that none made in his image and likeness be lost. Therefore, he relentlessly and tirelessly pursues us. God's son Jesus came to restore wholeness to our world. He came to give us himself, the Word who dwells among us.

Just as God never gives up on us, so we must never give up on others, including ourselves. Our society rejects so many peoples, nations and individuals. Earlier generations respected the elderly for their wisdom and experience of life. But now they are often relegated to rest homes, back bedrooms and institutions. Often whole groups of people have been cast aside or stereotyped as lazy, unproductive or useless to society, only because of their skin color, ethnic origin or religion. They are rejected as a group, out of hand, with little recourse for rebuttal. Society often shuns certain individuals, for little reason. Some people are ignored because they don't fit in, perhaps because of a handicap, a language barrier or a political disagreement. Each day we may see peoples and individuals being rejected. But we huddle together with the ninety-nine in the safety of the fold, instead of reaching out to the one who is lost.

What might be the saddest of all is those of us who give up on ourselves. We feel that we are not smart enough, attractive enough or athletic enough. We think that everyone surpasses us, while we don't measure up. We retreat to the privacy and security of our own little world. We won't venture out because danger surrounds us. When we give up on ourselves, we've lost almost everything.

Even though society operates on majority rule, this should never mean that we give up on others. When we give up on others we lose the richness of what they can offer. Their gift of themselves adds to our wholeness. To reject others, their opinions and works, causes the loss of much good in our world. Wc should foster the attitude displayed by the Lord. Not only do we need to reach out, but to go out and search for the lost and rejected of our world. We need to show that we care by doing our best to see that none will be lost. Our deeds need not be heroic, but they must be sincere and profound. In our own way, whatever it may be, let us seek out the lost and rejected. Let us show God's love and respect to others today.

Look to the Heart

Society glamorizes appearances. Fashion magazines tout the latest fashions. Television commercials advertise the current look in hairstyles, cosmetics and food. They entice us to look our best and dress with class. These voices encourage us to impress others with how we look and act. Our job, our influence and our friends all seem to depend on our appearance. Society values only those who will get ahead and prosper.

What God values in human beings is very different from what society values. The Hebrew Scriptures recount the story of how Samuel chose David to replace Saul as King of Israel. The Lord told Samuel to go to Jesse of the tribe of Benjamin. The anointed of the Lord would spring from Jesse's sons. The eldest son, Eliab, paraded before Samuel. He was strong and handsome. Certainly, thought Samuel, this is the anointed of the Lord. But God cautioned the prophet, "Do not look on his appearance or on the height of his stature, because I have rejected him; for the Lord sees not as man sees; man looks on the outward appearance, but the Lord looks on the heart" (1 Sam 16:7). As God's plan unfolded it became clear that the Lord chose David, who would solidify the kingdom of Israel and lead it to greatness.

The story of David challenges us to look beyond appearances and gaze into the heart. A flashy suit, a new hairstyle or designer jeans may attract our attention, but they need not dominate our powers of judgment. Too often we allow what we see, smell or hear to sway us. We seem unable to look deeply enough to see what glows in a person's heart and character. It is difficult to see another's character, because it takes time and we live in an impatient world. We often can't be bothered to take the time to look into the heart. It never hurts to look good, but this cannot be the final judgment as to our own worth and merit or the way we judge others.

If we can gaze into the heart, then with time we can see people's goodness. The Scriptures tell us that David was a shepherd; he needed time to display the qualities of a king. Through his alliance with Jonathan, David received enough time, and the people accepted him. Likewise, we need to give others the time and space they need to show us their capabilities. In this way we can look into their hearts, discover their characters and act accordingly.

Let's not allow society's anxiety about charm and appearances to deceive us. As God cautioned Samuel, let us be warned to take the time to look deeper into those we meet, to discover the beauty of character which flows from the heart. Therein lies the true beauty of the person. Therein rests the presence of God.

Express Your Feelings

We live in a world where the perfect lures us. We seek the perfect game in baseball or the perfect diamond in gems. Body builders strive to create the ideal physique or figure and the flawless line and muscle tone. The perfect is valued to such an extent that it often becomes the standard, the only acceptable result.

It's unfortunate that perfection is so desirable, because the perfect is so rare. We might make a career of baseball and never play a perfect game. We could search the gem mines of the world and never find a perfect diamond. We could spend all our energy in exercise and never fashion a perfect muscle line. Why then does perfection attract us?

I think the answer may lie in the brokenness which flaws our world. Most of us have a difficult time accepting the blemishes we see in our world, in others and especially in ourselves. We want to believe that the brokenness and fragility are illusions, and that perfection lurks just around the corner. We fear seeing the world as it is. We are afraid to look into the mirror and see our own image. We don't want to believe that we fall short. We have been told that men don't cry and women don't get angry. We suppress our feelings because we feel ashamed to show our fragility to others.

Jesus was perfect in his earthly existence, yet he openly showed his feelings. When the traders desecrated the house of God, Jesus did not heed society's standards, which said that a man of Jesus' stature, a rabbi, could not show outrage (cf. Jn 2:13-17). When his friend Lazarus died Jesus was not afraid to weep so that others might know how much he loved his friend (cf. Jn 11:35). Jesus was not afraid to show disappointment in his chosen leader Peter when the apostle denied him three times (cf. Lk 22:54-62). The perfect one displayed what society often frowns on: his emotions.

Jesus the teacher gives us a lesson in his ability to show his humanity. He shows us the goodness of all the aspects of our humanity. To be angry, to cry and to show disappointment might be a sign of weakness to society, but to God it only shows the reality of the human condition. Some people believe that brokenness should be hidden. Perhaps they have never heard of the fall and original sin. The world makes demands and presents us with many different obstacles. To deny the reality of the world is to deny our humanity. To deny our humanity is to deny the process of creation which God continues to display. Creation continues as our world evolves. Creation continues as the human condition and reality change over time.

The perfect may be an ideal for which we strive, but it need not be our ultimate goal. Jesus understands the human condition and asks us to strive toward perfection with the understanding that we will never quite make it. Let us accept our brokenness, our fragility and our humanity. Let us accept our world, others and ourselves as we strive for the best despite our shortcomings.

The Greatest Gift

As we grow older, we learn to value different types of gifts. As children, we thrill over that special doll, the fastest toy car or the most sophisticated electronic game. As adolescents and young adults, we think we have a better understanding of gifts. We look for the best clothes or the flashiest car. As adults our ideas about gifts mature. Possibly we begin to look at more practical and valuable things such as needed work clothes or an investment for the future.

Most people probably think of a gift as something that we don't presently have but would like to possess. People ask us to make a Christmas or birthday list of the things we need. Out of generosity and love we buy gifts for those we care about. It is a treasured and exciting way to show another how much we care. Sharing our surplus with others expresses the importance we place on our relationships with the people we love.

As strange as it might seem to our society, the best gifts cannot be purchased. We normally have them with us, but seem to notice them only when they're gone. Friendships are a great gift that we often take for granted. We seldom think about our health until we get sick, and then we ask, "Why me?" Faith is another gift which does not command much attention. This gift is like a seed planted by God through baptism. It needs to be nurtured through the waters of life in order to grow and bear fruit. When misfortune, injury or death tests our faith, we can then see if that seed planted so long ago has matured enough to sustain us. If it is too weak, then our faith will be snuffed out at the slightest opposition.

Like all the best gifts we can possess, the greatest gift of all cannot be purchased, but is ours for the asking. All gifts can be tarnished or destroyed, even those special gifts that we receive from loved ones, and the free gifts of friendship, health and faith. But one gift can never be damaged, defiled or broken. It is the gift of salvation, eternal life with God. Through the mercy of God we have found new birth, "we have been born anew to a living hope through the resurrection of Jesus Christ from the dead, and to an inheritance which is imperishable, undefiled, and unfading, kept in heaven for you, who by God's power are guarded through faith for a salvation ready to be revealed in the last time" (1 Pet 1:3b-5). Nothing can diminish or tarnish God's gift of salvation to the human race. Jesus through his death and resurrection has won for us the gift beyond all others. We may rarely think about it, but it is the only gift which gives our lives on earth true meaning.

Salvation costs nothing in a material sense and is available to all. But we seldom think in such terms. Instead of worrying about the quality of the next gift we purchase for another, let us give the best gift we can offer to anyone—our faith. Expressed in so many simple ways, faith shared with another can bestow the gift of God. Faith shared with another moves our world closer to salvation, the gift of God that surpasses all others.

Do You Love Me?

Jesus asked Peter, "Simon, son of John, do you love me?" (Jn 21:15). We remember these words from the end of John's Gospel. Jesus asked Peter the same question three times, "Do you love me?" The three questions paralleled the three denials of Peter. But there is more. Jesus not only asks "do you love me," but "do you love me more than these? Do you love me sufficiently to pay the price, to give your life for me?"

When we reflect on Jesus' question it seems so easy and simple to say, like Peter, "Lord, you know everything; you know that I love you" (Jn 21:17). But if this is true, how do we show this love in a world which daily hungers for the love of God? Can we express our true feelings or has the world with its callousness choked off the love which God calls forth from within us?

Jesus' question to Peter challenges all of us.

The challenge comes from asking ourselves whether we love enough to pay the price. It is relatively easy to say that we love the Lord when it costs us nothing, when it is convenient or even expedient in certain situations. When difficult times overtake us, when it may cost us our reputation, our status or position, are we equally able to proclaim Jesus as Lord and say, "Yes, Lord, you know that I love you!"

Like Peter, most of us probably need a conversion experience in order to love the Lord without limit. Peter let fear overcome him on the night before Jesus died. Peter denied the Lord, quaking at the slightest hint that he might be one of Jesus' disciples. Yet, in Jesus' Easter appearance at the Sea of Galilee, we hear how Peter, with his confession of faith, is told that he will die at the hands of others because of his belief in the Lord (cf. Jn 21:18). Somehow the miracle of the resurrection has brought Peter to unconditional faith. We can read in the Acts of the Apostles how his faith catalyzed the formation of Judeo-Christianity.

We need to experience the conversion which Peter found in his life. Only through conversion can we love without counting the cost. Only through conversion can we pay the price. God has given us our lives to be used for building up the kingdom of

God. The kingdom is built with love lived through action. Action may cost us a friend, money or position. This is the price of which Jesus spoke when he asked Peter, "Do you love me more than these?" The price may be all that we are or could be. But the reward is eternal life with God.

Each day Jesus calls us by name, "Do you love me?" Each day we answer, "Yes," but sometimes we are not able or willing to pay the price. The question challenges us to find the answer that leads to life. It is the Lord Jesus calling, "Come follow me!"

God Consoles Us

Unfortunately, suffering, invades our everyday life. Sometimes physical pain strikes, when we fall sick or get injured. The most common form of suffering is psychological. This may be the worst form, since it may not appear that anything is wrong. People in such a position often suffer alone. If others are unaware of our suffering, they can't reach out and lend a helping hand, a sympathetic word or an open ear. We feel alone and abandoned, as if no one cares.

The natural reaction for many who suffer is to ask "why me?" Good Christians think how much better they could serve God and God's people if they were free of pain, whether physical or mental. We think of the time that seems wasted when we cannot do all the things we would like to do. Such a situation can lead to self-pity and a sour outlook on life. People who know us well can sense instantly that something is wrong. They want to help but don't know where to begin. Self-pity makes us weigh on others.

St. Paul knew all about suffering, as did his model for life, Jesus. Paul was imprisoned several times, shipwrecked, chased out of town, slandered and eventually martyred. Paul realized that the many Christian communities which he had formed suffered along with him. Being a good judge of human nature, Paul knew where people's suffering could lead. He did not want Christians to drown in self-pity. He wanted his brothers and sisters in Christ to express the optimism which flows from the knowledge that God acts in the world.

Paul must have especially cherished the Corinthians. He traveled to Corinth several times and spent a significant amount of time there. Many Scripture scholars today say that 2 Corinthians is a composite of several letters. This means that Paul wrote the community numerous times (not merely twice as might be thought from the canonical 1 and 2 Corinthians). He answered questions and urged the people to live their newly acquired faith to the fullest. In the midst of the answers and the encouragement, Paul gave the people a wonderful promise, "Our hope for you is unshaken; for we know that as you share in our sufferings, you will also share in our comfort" (2 Cor 1:7). Suffering may come our way, but God's consolation will ultimately overcome any problems or obstacles which we may encounter.

The promise which St. Paul gave to the Christian community at Corinth consoles us as well. God is there for us now and always will be, just as he has always been there for all peoples at all times. The challenge is to turn to God in our suffering and allow him to bear the burden. Thereby, he will release us from what seems so hard to bear. God stands ready to wrap each one of us in a blanket of consolation which dries all tears, cures all ills and lifts all burdens. If we can believe that Jesus abides with us as he promised, then we can be certain that our brother, friend and Lord waits, ready to meet our needs.

Suffering will come but God will console us. While it may seem to drag on forever, suffering will end. But God's consolation is infinite. When feeling down, troubled or when suffering in any way, remember that God waits for us with a heart of love and consolation that has no bounds.

The Power of Faith

Who doesn't enjoy having a sense of power? Some feel power in a physical sense, such as the baseball player who smacks a ball over the centerfield fence, or the hefty fullback who tramples would-be tacklers in a quest for the end zone. Most people probably experience power in a less aggressive but still significant way. In talking with friends, colleagues or business associates we feel a sense of power when we can persuade another to try our way of doing things. We exhilarate in a sense of power when others look up to us and hang on what we say.

The greatest power that one can experience doesn't come through physical might or influence on others. No, the power that is most profound and most important for all humanity comes from faith. With faith we can move mountains; with faith the sycamore can be uprooted and transplanted into the sea (cf. Lk 17:6). Faith gives us strength because it gives us freedom. Faith liberates us from our slavery to society and all that this world asks of us. Faith especially frees us from being slaves to the law.

In his letters to the Romans and Galatians, St. Paul extols the benefit of faith over the law. "Before faith came, we were confined under the law, kept under restraint until faith should be revealed" (Gal 3:23). In other words, the law was our monitor until Christ came to bring about our justification through faith. But now that faith has arrived, we are no longer in the monitor's charge (cf. Gal 3:24-25). Faith frees us to comply with the law, not as slaves, but as children of God seeking to return to the one from whom we came. As with human law, the laws of God are meant to organize and guide us to greater harmony, not to choke off our life or put obstacles in our way. With the aid of outside people and guides, faith gives us the power to direct our lives toward God, both as manifest today and in eternal life.

Faith is often thought of in terms of a mere concept, something we possess in a passive manner. But active faith forms the most forceful and efficacious display of power that we can give the world. We demonstrate such faith in our lives of discipleship and Christian service. Throughout history, people with strong faith have moved nations, changed attitudes and promoted Christian ideals.

The strength of faith can fill our lives and only needs to be nurtured. People, events and nature all help to make our faith grow. As faith grows, its power increases and makes a difference in our lives. An expression reminds us that power corrupts, and this may be the case unless we use our faith wisely and for the good of all. Faith is a special gift of God. It needs to be applied to generate a power to convert the non-believer, encourage the sinner and be present with the broken hearted. Faith dispels the darkness of fear and casts out the ignorance of doubt. Let us use the greatest of all powers, our faith, to make God more present as we build the kingdom of God in today's world.

Responding to God

We believe that the presence of God surrounds us. The eyes of faith see God in all things. We can see God in nature, in the beauty of a sunrise, the power of an ocean storm or the gentle coolness of a soft summer breeze. We can see God in events, in the day-to-day occurrences, the ecstasies, high points and successes, as well as the low points and failures. God is especially present in our family, friends and loved ones, our business associates and colleagues, our neighbors and community acquaintances. God is present even in those people we don't like or don't even know.

How do we respond to the presence of God in our lives? Do we recognize the presence of God or do we allow God to pass us by? The sinful woman who welcomed Jesus when he dined at the Pharisee's home recognized the presence of God (cf. Lk 7:36-50). Luke says that the woman washed Jesus' feet with her tears and dried them with her hair. She then kissed the Lord's feet and anointed them with perfumed oil. This unnamed woman responded to God's presence by showing special love. Because of her action and her loving response to God, Jesus said that her many sins were forgiven.

We encounter the presence of God each day in many ways. But I suspect that we dismiss most of these encounters as routine and trivial. We hope to find God in the supernatural and, in the process, we fail to notice the natural presence of the Lord. What opportunities we miss in passing by the presence of God!

God's presence often challenges us. A panhandler may ask us for spare change as we walk down the street. How do we respond? We may give some money or we may pass on. But whatever we choose to do, how do we respond to the challenge of God before us? Do we become angry? Are we frustrated that this child of God chose to ask me for help?

Hopefully our attitude is more loving. Jesus responded positively to the woman who had shown him kindness and love. Can we show the kind of love that the unnamed woman of St. Luke's Gospel showed Jesus?

God comes to us in hidden and varied ways. If we recognize God's presence in nature or in people, how do we respond? We may find God every day, but it is never ordinary. When we recognize the presence of God in whatever form it may take, we need to respond with all our mind and strength. When meeting a friend the golden rule may suffice, but when we encounter God we need to make the extra effort and go the extra mile. Jesus went the extra mile for us when he carried the cross to Calvary and suffered a horrible death so that we could have life.

God comes in many ways. Are we watching? God will somehow become manifest in the beauty, events and personalities of this day. When we find God, let us rejoice and respond. Let our encounter with the living God bring us to greater heights of joy.

Perseverance in God

Things don't always go the way we plan. We set out a long range scheme for our lives which ends up in twists, turns and reversals, instead of the straight line we originally envisioned. Even on a daily basis things sometimes become muddled and confused. The best plans can go awry when events or people spoil the neat arrangement we had worked out. When things do not work out as expected, it is only natural to feel discouraged, to throw our hands up and to cry out in utter despair, "Why should I continue; why should I plan?" But such defeatism is an evil which lurks to ensnare us.

Throughout human history, things have not worked out as planned. The Israelites did not plan on spending four hundred and fifty years in bondage in Egypt, but the exodus united them as a chosen people. Mary did not plan to be the mother of God, but her fiat helped bring salvation to our world. St. Paul did not plan on being the apostle to the gentiles, but his encounter with Jesus on the road to Damascus transformed his life, and ultimately ours as well. Often, unexpected events can brighten our future, if we have the courage to persevere.

From his own experience St. Paul knew the necessity of perseverance. His own suffering and trials never dampened his zeal. He once wrote, "We are afflicted in every way, but not crushed; perplexed, but not driven to despair; persecuted, but not forsaken; struck down but not destroyed" (2 Cor 4:8-9). Paul knew that setbacks would come and that things would often not work out as planned. But God never abandons us and so we should never despair. We can never be crushed or destroyed.

Perseverance helps us to continue despite the pain, and to look beyond the present to what could be. It makes us realize that the world has not destroyed us. Perseverance gives us the inner drive and dynamism to keep going. Jesus applauded such tenacity in his description of the persistent widow and her claims against the corrupt judge (Lk 18:1-8). We need to push forward in our lives, and never to remain complacent or stagnant. Lived in the spirit of God, perseverance makes things happen in our world. In the end it will reap huge dividends.

Faced with many obstacles, we struggle to persevere in our endeavors. The original sin of our world makes life tough and demands perseverance. Young people find it difficult to stay in school, and adults sometimes struggle to keep pace at work. But as St. Paul has told us, if we persevere we will always win out, for God's presence will strengthen and sustain us. If discouragement sets in when things don't seem to go the way we had planned, let us strive harder to persevere and experience God in the process.

What Profit the World?

Today's society revolves around profit. The business world especially aims to make money, since without it industry cannot continue to operate. So profit can be a good insofar as it allows progress and provides jobs for many workers. Profitability can be a personal concept as well. Do my actions profit others? Do my work and my being make a positive contribution to society? Much of our self-esteem often hinges on acceptability, which can translate into the measure of profit we can fulfill or gain for ourselves and others.

Profit for members of God's family must mean more than production of goods, services or money. Profit for the Christian must mean how one advances in life on a path that leads back to God, the Creator and source of our life. Most people think little about our value in the eyes of God, but therein lies the problem which besets many people today.

Jesus warned his disciples about this. "For what does it profit a man, to gain the whole world and forfeit his life?" (Mk 8:36). We may grow rich in many ways, such as status, power or possessions. Jesus' question challenges us to say, "What profit does the world hold for me?" If we think that this world holds more for us than our heavenly home, then we most certainly will destroy ourselves and miss the goal for which we were created.

Profit in today's society is not evil but fulfills a good purpose. Still, these earnings must be tempered with the spiritual profit which leads us to what St. Paul calls the higher realms (cf. Col 3:1-2). The income we make in the world is good as long as it aids our growth and advancement in the spiritual life. If all that the world can produce leads us only to greater heights now, with no thought about our spiritual home, then all such gain produces nothing fruitful in the eyes of God.

Do the profits of society draw me closer to God or keep me at a distance? This is the key question. If what we earn helps us to see or experience the presence of God, then our true gain is to advance along the road which leads to life. But if what we gain keeps God at a distance, then we need to reconsider the value of such profit. Jesus has told us that the kingdom of God is like a valuable pearl, which merchants will sell everything they own to obtain. Should we not take a similar attitude and renounce any profit which leads us astray from the true goal of this life? Money cannot buy eternal life.

What profit is the world? Life challenges us

daily with this question. We need to honestly look at our lives and see if the profits of society aid or hinder our search for God. When we find the answer, then we need the courage to act on it. The world provides all the good things given to us by God. Let us use them wisely so as to gain eternal life with God.

Give Your Life to God

A common mindset today assumes that the one life I have is mine and so I must use it as I see fit. But Christianity speaks of a different reality. Our life does not belong to us. Life is a gift from God. We must give our life back to God.

St. John in his Gospel often uses metaphors to illustrate ideas. In chapter 12 we read, "Truly, truly, I say to you, unless a grain of wheat falls into the earth and dies, it remains alone; but if it dies, it bears much fruit. He who loves his life loses it, and he who hates his life in this world will keep it for eternal life" (12:24-25). The seed represents our life. Unless we die for others and God, we produce no fruit. But when we give our lives freely, we find life and produce much fruit.

Jesus exemplified the paradox of losing one's life in order to truly gain eternal life. In his own suffering and death, Jesus showed us the way that leads to life. The seed was Jesus. He died for us and so merited eternal life for all of us. As with all paradoxes, the paradox of the cross puzzles us. St. Paul called it a stumbling block for some, but for those of us who believe it became the path to salvation (cf. 1 Cor 1:23-24).

Jesus does not ask many of us to make the supreme sacrifice and give our physical lives for him or others. That might be easier since it would only take a moment. The decision would be made and it would be final. But Jesus does ask us to give who we are and share ourselves with others. Parents probably know this best in the way that they sacrifice themselves, their dreams, their time and energy for their children. Most parents do this willingly. Instead of looking on it as a burden, they accept it as a part of life.

The example of Jesus or the example of a good parent gives us a model for our lives. Perhaps yesterday we needed to give ourselves to our neighbor. Possibly today a member of our family will need us. Tomorrow it may be a colleague or business associate who asks for help. It is not easy. Nothing worthwhile in life usually is. Yet the fruit produced through self-giving enriches us tremendously.

Dying to others makes the kingdom come alive in our world. The paradox of the cross lived day by day is the mustard seed which grows into the biggest bush or the yeast which makes the whole dough rise (cf. Lk 13:18-21). Death can seem so negative and without hope. Yet like the seed that dies and produces much fruit, death will usher us into eternal life with God.

Let us share the kingdom and lose our lives for others. Then we will find happiness in this world and eternal joy in the world to come.

God Abides with Us

God Loves Us Always

Could we today give the most precious gift we have to the Lord? Would we be able to give our whole life and especially our hearts to Jesus? With its ability to love, the heart makes us different from other creatures, and special in all God's creation. Can we offer that gift to God?

Jesus gave us his heart without reservation. He asked no questions and demanded no payment. He simply and completely gave himself to us, asking nothing in return. When Jesus walked to his death along the road to Calvary he did not ask his followers to do just as he did. Jesus knew that most of us would be incapable of such devotion. Yet, he showed through his example that faith can conquer fear. Along the way he encouraged others: Simon of Cyrene, Veronica the woman of faith, and the women of Jerusalem who watched his march to death.

Jesus has suffered so much, both physically through crucifixion and by the many sins against his Sacred Heart. One might think it only natural that he would pull back his love from those who have shown no sign of remorse or desire to do better. We cannot understand the mind of God. As St. Paul wrote in Romans, "O the depth of the riches and wisdom and knowledge of God! How unsearchable are his judgments and how inscrutable his ways" (11:33). One might think that God might withdraw his heart and his love from us, but this is not possible.

"For the gifts and the call of God are irrevocable" (Rom 11:29). St. Paul has clearly stated what is so hard for us to believe. The offenses which God must endure from sinful humanity would sour any ordinary person. But God is anything but ordinary. God is infinite, beyond all our greatest imaginations and thoughts. God is too full of love to allow the pettiness of humanity to distract him from his desire to guide us to heaven.

When we consider that nothing can take God's

love from us, we must reflect on how we react to others when they do things that offend us. Certainly as humans the insensitivity or ingratitude of others causes us pain. We react instinctively. But if we look at the example of God, who is so offended yet continues to show love through it all, then we can find another way to react to the pain that others inflict upon us. Are we big enough to return love for pain, imitating God who loves us beyond all that we can imagine?

God loves us and will never revoke that love. Can we say the same in our relations with others? If nothing can separate us from God's love (cf. Rom 8:35-39), then we should not allow ourselves to be separated from the love of others. Let us take seriously Paul's reminder that God's love and call are irrevocable. Let us pass on a similar blessing to all we meet today.

Peace through Surrender

As I walked home today via the lake path, the beauty of the day spoke to me of God's goodness. After a long winter darkened by gray skies, I welcomed the warmth of the afternoon sunshine. A note of spring filled the air. I could see the buds on the trees and shrubs, and along the lake front daffodils and tulips danced in the breeze. Even the birds had returned. The cardinals and the robins sang, the jay screamed and the woodpecker drilled on an unsuspecting oak. The squirrels and the chipmunks had risen from their winter naps and were out in force, scampering under a bush at my approach. It was evident that the hand of God was directing the scene before me. This was God's gift to me.

Ever since the day I told God I would follow him, every day has been as wonderful as that spring day along the lake. Despite rain, blizzards and bitter cold, the Spirit of the living God within me glows brightly. My whole life burns with the fire of the Holy Spirit. The enthusiasm that I have for my daily tasks has taken a giant step forward ever since I asked Jesus to help me with my burdens. I surrendered to him and he brought me to fulfillment. What miraculous results flowed from my submission of self!

Life has its ups and downs, but surrendering to Jesus will sustain us. Our modern, secular society incites us to struggle for control. But surrender is the path to peace. Day-to-day existence through work, relationships, recreation and home life take on their true meaning when Christ lives at the center of our lives. Things then seem to go better because through Jesus we have come to that special interior peace which only he can give, an interior peace which soothes the rough times, highlights the good and brings continuity to life.

When we surrender our thoughts and desires to the Lord, then and only then can we begin to experience the peace of the Spirit, the Spirit of the Risen Christ in our daily lives.

In the Hands of God

The Scriptures, particularly the Old Testament, abound in images of Yahweh God caring for the Israelites, holding them in his hands, guiding them and carrying them whenever necessary. In Isaiah God reassures us, "I have graven you on the palms of my hands" (Is 49:16). These images speak just as strongly to us today as they did to the Jewish people long before the time of Christ.

I suspect that if we honestly thought about it, we could recall special times in our lives when we felt the hand of God guiding us. Forks in the road of life show evidence of God's presence. We always wonder about the road not taken, yet we live our lives based on decisions made at these forks. The image of God assisting the Israelites in their exodus from Egypt speaks to us today in times of decision. "The Lord your God who goes before you will himself fight for you, just as he did for you in Egypt before your eyes, and in the wilderness, where you have seen how the Lord your God bore you, as a man bears his son, in all the way that you went until you came to this place" (Deut 1:30-31). We know that God has been carrying us, but often realize it only after the fact. Like the Israelites, we fail to see God's presence in the happenings of our lives. We only realize the gentle touch of God in retrospect; we miss the Lord's personal touch.

Psalm 131 relates the image of God to a mother feeding her children. "I have calmed and quieted my soul, like a child quieted at its mother's breast; like a child that is quieted is my soul" (Ps 131:2). In speaking to the Israelites, the Psalmist exhorts us as well to place our life in God's hands.

The prophecy of Isaiah encouraged the Israelites in exile and still exhorts us to allow God into our lives. "[You] have been borne by me from your birth, carried from the womb; even to your old age I am he, and to gray hairs I will carry you" (Is 46:3b-4). How often have we said, "I can make it on my own; I don't need you!" We could not be more foolish than to reject help from God. Our only assurance of success in any endeavor comes with and through God.

Although we have made incredible progress in many things since the time of the Israelites, we still have not learned that we are in good hands with God. We must be open to the gentle touch of God in our lives. When we allow the Spirit of God room to operate, miraculous events occur as we ride in the palm of his hand.

My Best Friend

I am lucky. I have a best friend. We know all too well that friends come and go in this world. We are fortunate if we have two or three close friends in our whole life, people we can truly count on. But I am certain that my friend will always be with me.

Best friends are a lifetime treasure. Friendships like this can only come about through total commitment, sharing and self-sacrifice. Friends help each other and are always present when needed. Best friends challenge us and help us grow. Best friends smooth our rough edges and make us more human to ourselves and others.

My best friend is truly special. Whenever I have a problem my companion is there. My friend listens and offers advice. I am never without my best friend, even when we are not physically together. We have built a relationship that transcends our physical presence. We are constantly present to each other in thought and understanding. My best friend is only a heart beat away at any moment.

My best friend is not unique to me but is a solace to many. Everyone who welcomes my friend is made a friend as well. Hospitality, openness and a willingness to love is all that my friend asks. You, too, can have my friend as your best friend. All you need do is ask.

My best friend is God. God never fails but is ever present. God challenges me while we converse in prayer. I might not get all the answers my way, but that is all right. It often seems that God gives me better things than what I ask for. God knows what he is doing!

Thank you, God, for being my best friend. You are my best friend because no matter what, no matter when, I can always count on you. You will always be alongside me. Teach me to follow you more closely so that our friendship can grow and mature. Help me to lead others to you so they too can have the best friend in the world.

The Voice of the Spirit

How often have you felt unable to speak in certain situations, only to surprise yourself at what came out of your mouth? The busy and complex world in which we live calls us to action on many occasions. We are asked to give a word of encouragement to one or to offer a gesture of sympathy to another. Often people come to us expecting that we can give them some good advice. Although it is natural to want to help those who ask us something, it is also quite normal to feel inadequate. So we may shy away from situations which ask us to speak. We are afraid that we won't know what to say and we fear that we may say the wrong thing.

The voice of God's Spirit is present in our world and will help us when we call. In his humanity Jesus knew of the timidity that can befall us. Thus he told his disciples, "What you are to say will be given to you in that hour; for it is not you who speak, but the Spirit of your Father speaking through you" (Mt 10:19-20). God's Spirit will inspire us with the right words or indicate the need for silence, as the situation dictates. We will be amazed at how God takes over when our own abilities are stretched beyond their capacity.

Trust fosters a climate where God's Spirit can operate. We must be open to the possibilities of God in our life. God will not force himself upon us or into situations, but waits for our invitation. Certainly God is always present, waiting to hear our call. Yet, through free will we have the privilege of saying yes or no to that help. If we are open and willing to let him act, then God's Spirit will take over at those difficult times. It need not be at a time of persecution as Jesus' words to his disciples indicate. God will aid us whenever we call. We will be amazed at what we say. Then we will realize that it was not us at all. No, God only used our voice to pronounce his word, a word that will meet the need at hand. If we cannot trust, if we fear to invite God into our lives, then we will be left alone to speak our own inadequate words. Without God's Spirit to guide us we will feel empty and inadequate. It will be mere coincidence that we might say something that will aid another in need. Openness to God will assure that the words we speak are not ours, but rather the Spirit of God speaking through us.

Life places us in situations which call us to say a good word to someone. Often our natural reaction is to draw back since we don't know what to say. How can we respond to the untimely death of a relative or close friend? What words can console the victim of crime? How can we soothe a heart torn by rejection? By ourselves we falter, but if we trust God, the Spirit will provide us with whatever we need. Let us not fear to respond to the many calls we receive. Let us speak as best we can, having the confidence that God's Spirit will give us the right words to say.

Acceptance

God offers us total acceptance and unconditional love. We could imagine God saying, "I accept you the way you are. I don't expect anything special but only desire what you give me today. I love you the way you were yesterday and I love you today. I will love you tomorrow. Acceptance means I love you now and will always love you.

"I think of you constantly and each thought shines with its own special beauty. When I think of you I remember all the wonderful times we have had, all the experiences we have shared. We share all, including our lives. But sharing isn't possible unless one has learned to accept the other, as they are, with no strings attached. That is how I love you.

"When our relationship gets strained I know we

will be reconciled. Our reunion always makes our bond stronger. Love solidifies our relationship and makes us one. I'm happy when we can talk and straighten things out. Our communication is honest and straightforward. Our relationship improves when we can talk.

"When you are troubled, bewildered or faced with difficulties I want to help. Just let me know and I will respond. I might not be able to be there in the way you desire, but I will be there nevertheless. I will never abandon you. You are precious to me and I love you. I accept you totally and unconditionally. All you need do is ask and I will answer. Be patient and have faith that all will work out.

"I am your best friend and relationships like that should never die. They need to be nurtured and watered so fruit can bud forth. My grace surrounds you like a dense cloud. Let it penetrate you. Don't try to run away. I am with you. You can always count on that.

"I am your God. I created you out of love. You are my child, so you can never escape from my love. I accept you as you are and you must accept me. Ours is a bond which can never be broken. I am your Father and Mother. I care for you; I accept you. Have faith my child, for I will always be with you!"

Fidelity

Like mortar which cements the bricks in a wall, fidelity holds our life together. We want to remain faithful to our commitments—to family, to friends and to our work. If we have made commitments in the community we want to remain faithful. Are we as faithful to God? Do we value such fidelity?

God is ever faithful to humanity. Despite their lack of faith, God guided and directed the Hebrews to the promised land which flowed with milk and honey. God sent prophets to encourage and exhort the people. The Father sent Jesus, God incarnate, to live among us and to die for us. God is ever faithful. As we read in 2 Timothy 2:11-13, "If we have died with him, we shall also live with him; if we endure, we shall also reign with him; if we deny him, he also will deny us; if we are faithless, he remains faithful, for he cannot deny himself."

God demonstrates his faithfulness to us in many ways. God is faithful in his presence, which enters our lives in many ways. It comes in the beauty of the sunrise and the sunset, in the gentleness of a summer breeze, and even in the roar of traffic. God is present in the stillness of a whisper and the tenderness of a smile or hug. Are we present to God? Can he count on us? When God or God's people need us are we willing to stop and be present? Are we willing to interrupt our lives for others?

God is faithful in caring for all of us and never ceases to direct our lives. God nurtures us as a mother nurtures her infant. Do we care for others? Do we meet the needs of others: our children, members of our family, loved ones, those whom God sends into our lives?

God leads us by faith. Baptism ignited the spark of faith in us. But God constantly gives us opportunities to increase and nurture our faith. Do we use these opportunities? Or do we let them pass by and in the process miss God as well?

God is faithful in love. Having created us in love, God will never abandon us. St. Paul assures us that nothing can separate us from God's love. Are we equally faithful in our relationships? Can we love without reservation, qualification or reward? Have we been faithful to God recently?

God is ever faithful; what about us? God was faithful to the Hebrews. Jesus is faithful to us as the bread of life in the Eucharist. Let us be faithful to God and God's people in our caring presence, imitating in faith and love Jesus, our brother, friend and Lord.

God Lights Our World

God lights our world. God has given us the sun to rule the day. It brightens our world, giving light and warmth. The light that comes from candles and electric lights is still a gift of God, although made by humans, God's greatest creation. These inventions allow us to turn night into day at the touch of a switch. But as wonderful as the lights of our world are, the light of God which most pervades our world is love. God lights our world with his love, showering humanity in a bath of peace and tranquillity.

The love of God surrounds us. God's love resembles a single light bulb in the middle of a darkened room. Like the light from that bulb, the love of God radiates in all directions. Nothing can escape from God's love, although we might try to flee from it. As the Psalmist says, "Where shall I flee from your presence?" (Ps 139:7).

Just as the light of that single bulb gives warmth, so does divine love. That love bathes us in warmth. We can begin to understand the warmth of God's love in seeing how the sun heats the earth, a smile touches our hearts or a nourishing meal sustains our bodies. God's love gives warmth to our cold world.

The light of a single bulb helps us to find our way. With the aid of the light we can find our path and arrive at our destination. God's love works the same way. Guided by the loving hand of God we can find the path that leads to life. So many paths beckon us and so many forks in the road of life cross our path. Yet, only one leads to our home with God. But with the love of God in our hearts it is possible to avoid the potholes and dirt roads and find the super highway which Isaiah says leads to God. "A highway shall be there, and it shall be called the Holy Way" (Is 35:8).

The light of a single light bulb helps us to recognize others. Divine love enables us to see people better, including ourselves. With the love of God we can recognize situations that lead us astray from God. Similarly, we can use God's love as a guide to help others in their quest to find the correct road to life with God.

With God's love we have all we need. God's love surrounds us. It gives us warmth, direction and recognition. That love costs nothing since God gives it freely. Like all gifts, however, it must be accepted. Let us live in the warmth of God's love, accepting the greatest of all gifts and allowing it to bring us to eternal life.

Walking with the Lord

Have you ever wished that you could have walked with the Lord? Have you ever dreamed of a time machine whisking you back to Israel at the time of Jesus? How magnificent it would be to see, hear and walk with the Lord. As twentieth century people we would have a great advantage, knowing so much more about Jesus than those around us. We would know Jesus and recognize him—or would we?

Along the road to Emmaus two disciples of the Lord walked with Jesus all day, but they never recognized him (cf. Lk 24:13-35). They had walked his path, heard his words and witnessed his miracles. Why could they not recognize their companion that day as their friend and Lord, Jesus the Christ? Jesus explained the meaning of the Scriptures and told them of his life. Jesus enlightened the disciples' minds, but still they did not know with whom they walked. They recognized Jesus only in the breaking of the bread. Then their eyes were opened.

If those who had walked with Jesus for three years had difficulty in recognizing him, the same might be true for us, even with our two thousand years of knowledge and tradition. We probably would not know Jesus then, if we cannot see him now. We would not be able to walk as a disciple in Israel, if we cannot walk as one today.

How can I walk with the Lord? How can I witness to his works when he is not here? The simple answer to these questions is that Jesus is here. He abides with us. We need only open our eyes to his presence.

We walk with the Lord and we carry his standard when we walk with others with whom he would have walked. Jesus came to "preach good news to the poor...to proclaim release to the captives, and recovering of sight to the blind, to set at liberty those who are oppressed, to proclaim the acceptable year of the Lord" (Lk 4:18b-19). When we stand and walk with the poor, prisoners and those whom society has ostracized, we stand and walk with the Lord as well. We might not recognize the Lord face-to-face, but then neither did those disciples on the road to Emmaus. But we can recognize Jesus in the poor and the needy.

The Lord is present and we can walk with him. Our walk need not be a physical one. When we support those who have little, when we help the poor, then we walk with the Lord as if he were physically beside us. We need not turn back the clock. We can walk with Jesus today.

We all need to walk with the Lord. We do it by seeing Jesus' presence in the needs and problems of others. We walk with the Lord in our service to God's people. Let us help those who need us and walk with the Lord today.

God Is My Co-Pilot

We humans are a possessive lot. We cling with all our might to whatever we have. We growl, "It's mine" with such strength and authority that no one can doubt to whom a particular thing belongs. We do this with our clothes, our house, our car and even our life.

Remembering where all good things come from can give us a true perspective on life. God is the source of all good things, so in a real sense everything belongs to God. If we learn to release and to let go, then God can enter our lives. I think we would be amazed if we let God be our co-pilot.

Releasing control of our life certainly challenges most people. When we control our lives, we know precisely where we are, where we have been and where we intend to go. When we control things, we're sure that we know the outcome. But a moment's thought will show us that the illusion of control deceives us. We think we know what is best. But ultimately, God is in command. When we think we have control and things don't work out as we planned, we become angry and disappointed. But if we surrender and allow God to control our lives, then we do the will of God and receive what is best for us.

Surrender of our will and person to another makes great demands on us. Personal control makes us feel that we command our own lives. We need that feeling in a world which praises hard work and accomplishment. But when we allow God to direct our lives, when we surrender, then not only can God act more freely, but a great burden falls from our shoulders. The drive to accomplish things in our world doesn't torment us any longer.

God wants to be our co-pilot, but only waits for an invitation. God has given us intelligence and free will to help us live our lives properly. God doesn't ask us to negate our will and desire as humans, but only that we allow him to guide us toward those things we need but are often too blind to see.

If we let God help us, then our lives will be less complicated and more purposeful. We will accomplish our mission in this world with less anxiety. Let us allow God to be our co-pilot on the journey to eternal life.

Longing for God

Preparing to visit a loved one can be a fulfilling but hectic process. So much needs to be done. We need to pack. Some people find a checklist helpful, and mark off each item when it is safely stowed away. Some have traveled so frequently that they keep a fully stocked bag in their closet, ready for that trip which will soon come. Much emotion goes into preparing to see a loved one. Excitement runs high. For some it seems like a return to childhood. Like children anticipating Christmas or a birthday, our planned reunion fills all our thoughts. We channel all of our energy into our expectations. Soon we will be with the people we love. The anticipation seems to be as powerful as the reunion itself.

When we finally see the one for whom we long, a sense of calm descends on us. Waiting is over; now we can enjoy the presence of our special friend, relative, or spouse. For a moment the whole world seems to stand still. We savor the moment. Calm and serenity have replaced anxiety and longing. Once we attain our goal, we feel satisfied.

Preparations for visits with loved ones satisfy our temporal needs, but what about our needs which extend beyond time and space. How are we preparing to be with God? All of us long for God. Each time we recite the Lord's Prayer, we ask "thy kingdom come." Although we do long for God, most of us make few preparations. Few, if any of us, have our suitcase ready to go. We probably haven't even made a checklist. We want to walk in God's presence and be with God. But we often don't bother to prepare for it.

Longing for God demands preparation. When we prepare we must be in communication. We need to speak with our God, making known our needs and desires. We ought to have our things ready. This means that we must feel comfortable about our relationship with the Lord. Are we ready to journey to God or does unfinished business await us? If we truly live for God, if God is the goal of our life, then we must always be ready for our journey. Unlike our human reunions which can be more or less planned to our schedule, our reunion with the Lord comes on God's schedule, which seldom, if ever, coincides with our own.

As the source of our life and sustenance, God must be placed first when it comes to our preparations in this life. Anticipation, excitement and fulfillment are all part of our human reunions. They will be more fully realized in our reunion with God. As we long for the Lord, let us prepare so that when our scheduled reunion with God comes we will find the calm and peace we seek with God, the reason for our existence.

The Day of the Lord

People have been talking about the return of Jesus since the earliest Christian times. Known as the *Parousia* or more commonly as the second coming or the Day of the Lord, Jesus' return has attracted much attention. St. Paul focused on it in his letters to the Thessalonians. Paul and many others thought that the Lord would most certainly return soon, within the lifetime of those who knew Jesus in the flesh. People didn't speak much about the future and historians were not concerned with the past. The emphasis was on the present, for the Day of the Lord was coming and if people were not vigilant it would catch them off guard, "like a thief in the night" (1 Thess 5:2). But as we know, we have been waiting for nearly two thousand years and the Parousia is still only a hope. We continue to wait for the Lord.

Even though Jesus has not yet returned, in a sense the Day of the Lord has come. If we are observant, each day is the Day of the Lord. Our God is in all places and with all people except those who reject him. All is from God, and all is of God. We can be confident that the Day of the Lord was yesterday, is today and will be tomorrow. God comes each day with opportunities and challenges. These moments of grace draw the world and humanity closer together. Sometimes we miss the opportunities and reject the challenges. But God never gives up. Each day is the Lord's, and each day God comes in magnificent and often unexpected ways.

Sacred Scripture and Tradition typically describe the Day of the Lord as a terrifying and fearful event. God will judge each person. Everyone's life will be manifested for all to see. Certainly everyone must account to God for his or her life. How has that person used God's gifts and followed Jesus? As the light of our sun radiates in all directions and does not discriminate, so too the love of God, which comes from Jesus, the Light of the World, goes out to all. The love of God is with all except those who have chosen another god. Certainly God is everywhere except where God is not wanted. Without doubt the final Day of the Lord will be a terrifying experience for those who have chosen to live without God. People wonder what hell might be or where it is. Simply put, hell can only be where God is not wanted, for God's presence permeates all other places and beings.

Our greatest challenge comes daily. Each day we are asked to welcome the Lord and to make a place for him in our daily routine, often so busy and cluttered. We must remember that each day comes from God and belongs to the Lord. Since this reality calls us to daily commitment, we must welcome God's challenge and make a place for God in our day.

Today, this day of the Lord, let us welcome our God through prayer and word, through thought and action. Let God fill us and bring us closer to him this day.

A Sure Foundation

If you have been at sea during a storm, or watched the surf pound the shore, then you know and have experienced the power of the ocean. The sea can appear so gentle and calm, but its hidden power constantly threatens. It only needs to be disturbed to show its might.

When we have felt or seen the ocean's might, then we can better appreciate Jesus' image of a house on a rocky foundation (cf. Mt 7:24-27). Periodically we hear of how the invading ocean swallowed some beach front property. Sometimes we hear of homes on slopes which have slid to their ruin in the canyon below. In both cases the foundation was too weak to support the structure in the face of the elements. In one brief moment, the pounding surf and the relentless rains can shatter the dreams of a lifetime.

This image which Jesus used when teaching his apostles needs to be applied not only to homes and buildings, but to our lives. When Jesus said that the foolish person builds a house on sandy ground, he reminded us that at times we too have built on sand. Upon what or whom do we rely in our lives? Most of us could admit that the allurements and fascinations of the world have attracted us more than God. We might rely on our work which has become so important that it serves as a pseudo-god and the reason for our being. Some people build their lives on the false hopes and promises which the world gives. If we take this drug, all will seem fine and our worries will evaporate for a while. If we place our trust and confidence wholly on the empty promises of the secular world, then most certainly, as Jesus predicted, the house of our private little world will be destroyed.

We need a rock foundation. Such a base can

only be found with God. Jesus called Peter the rock. Jesus chose Peter as the foundation of the Church, and that foundation had to be solid. Even more fundamental for us is that Jesus is the rock, the foundation. He is the stone rejected by the builders which has become the cornerstone (cf. Lk 20:17). Thus, our lives must be firmly grounded and built upon the rock who is our God. If our lives are rooted in the Lord, then we'll stand fast even though the winds and the storms of life may pummel us.

Faith is the cement which connects us to God our rock. God has given us the spark of faith and now we must nurture it. With prayer and reflection we cement ourselves to God. With a life lived in loyalty to the teachings of Jesus, we continue to build upon the cornerstone. Let us be like Peter and accept Jesus' challenge to be rocks, both for ourselves and for others in spreading the good news of the Lord.

Discovering God Again

At certain times in life, we need to discover God anew. For many people God seems distant, impersonal and unapproachable. When problems arise and difficulties plague our life, it may seem that God doesn't care. But appearances and reality are two different things. W need to discover God again.

Although we may not realize it, God is personal and close to us. God is that best friend we have always sought. God is the one with whom we can totally share ourselves and our feelings. As our Creator, God knows us thoroughly, with our hopes, fears and the desires of our hearts. It makes sense to share ourselves with the one who knows us best. But we need to believe that God is near and listens to us. We realize this only when we discover that God is always present to us, and can be found in all places and with all peoples. God is here. We merely need to rediscover his presence.

God is found in the beauty of the sunrise, the gentleness of a soft breeze, and in the savage storm which pounds us with rain. God is especially present in people, in the warm smile, the pleasant "good morning" and the words of comfort. Since God is present in others, we need to rediscover this special presence and appreciate it for the benefits it brings. It is easy to see God in wondrous and magnificent things like the sunrise or the power of a storm. But we may miss God in the ordinary, especially in daily events and people. Yet, the mundane and ordinary dominate our lives and this must be the foundation for our discovery of God. If we can discover God again in the ordinary aspects of our life, then God can be discovered at all times and in all places. This is as it should be, since God is present to all, denying no one while embracing all.

We need to discover God again. Living within a society which looks for the exotic, it might surprise us to think that God is so imminent and dwells within us. Let us discover anew the God who is Creator, Redeemer and Sanctifier. Let us find God in all the things we do and all the people we meet this day.

Jesus Abides with Us

Being away from family and loved ones often challenges us. Sometimes we are separated from those we love through no choice of our own, perhaps due to military service, a business trip or a job change. Sometimes our own desires force us to separate, such as going away to college or going on an extended vacation. No one likes to be away from loved ones, but life can force it on us.

The most important person in our life is one who is always with us, although we sometimes fail to see him. During his time on earth, Jesus made many friends and preached the good news as he received it from the Father. With all the things that Jesus said and did, it isn't easy to pick out the one special promise he gave us, a promise that can never be taken away. But one does stand out: his promise to always abide with us. We know that salvation can be ours, but to attain it costs us our lives. God bestows the gift of faith on us when we become members of his family, yet faith is only active when we water the seed, allowing it to blossom.

Like the sun, we can always count on Jesus' presence. His final words to his disciples give us a special promise, "I am with you always" (Mt 28:20b). Like God's love, Jesus' presence can never be taken away or lost. It is certainly true that we often do not recognize Jesus' presence. We miss Jesus in others, especially those who might repel or challenge us, such as the poor, the handicapped, the sick and the aged. We might excuse ourselves for not finding Jesus in such people, since we may not meet them often. But do we believe that Jesus is present in the everyday, and that we can reach out to him at anytime, in any place, for any reason? It's sad to think that in our daily life we often don't recognize the best friend we have, who never leaves our side.

Nothing can fill the void that exists in our lives without the presence of God. The material world constantly beckons us to satisfy our wants with the things which money and power can purchase. We may enjoy these things for a while, but they will not last. It's like putting a new patch on old wineskins; the tear only becomes worse (cf. Mt 9:17).

Only Jesus gives meaning to life. When we find ourselves far from those we love, when the pain of loneliness invades our being, we can find the solution in Jesus. Can we find Jesus in others, in events, in time? Can we find Jesus in ourselves? When the times come—and they surely come for all of us—when we need someone special, let us enter inside ourselves to find the Lord, the one who is ever present, the one who will be with us until the end of the world!

God Lives in Each of Us

We know and believe that Jesus is present in our world. Before he ascended into heaven, he promised to be with us until the end of time (cf. Mt 28:20b). Yet, where do we find God? How does Jesus operate in our world? The unseen God is active, but in ways that seem mysterious and hidden most of the time.

Jesus, the Son of God, had a physical body during his time on earth. He felt pain and emotion as we do. Through the Incarnation God came and dwelt among us. The people of the apostolic era had a vivid sense of Jesus' presence. He was real to them, just as someone whom we knew but has died is real to us.

But what about those of us who live centuries after the time of Jesus? How is our Lord present to us today? The great 16th century mystic and religious reformer, St. Teresa of Avila, proposed the best solution that I have read. In a prayer she wrote, "Christ has no body on earth but yours, no hands or feet but yours. Yours are the eyes through which Christ looks with compassion for the world. Christ has no body on earth but yours." As the prayer states, we are Jesus' hands and feet. Our Lord dwells within us. The Incarnation did not cease after Jesus ascended to heaven. Jesus lives as much today as he did two thousand years ago. Jesus lives in us but we often do not recognize him.

If St. Teresa is correct, then we have a great responsibility. The God who dwells inside each one of us desires to be shared with others. This is only possible if we make ourselves available to do God's work. Jesus wants to help the poor, the rich and the handicapped. But he can only use our hands and feet to do the work. Only through our eyes can Jesus see and hear the plight of the people. Jesus wants to help the immigrant, the prisoner and the rejected and marginalized of society, but our Lord can only act if we are willing to act. Jesus acts when our hands and feet, our senses and our minds reach out in an effort to help others. Being the hands and feet of the Lord places an awesome responsibility on us.

Many people help others, but few realize that in the process they became God to those in need. If we act only out of duty or responsibility, then we cannot communicate the love of God to others. We might go through the motions mechanically, but our heart is not in it. People are served but the full benefit that God can bring is lost.

We need to remember that through the Incarnation, God dwells within us. Jesus' death upon the cross released us from bondage. It also made possible a unique role for humanity, carrying on God's work in the world. When a person or a situation calls for our attention, let us remember that we carry God within us. Let us bring all that we are and recognize that God lives within each of us. In this way we can serve the world better and make the unseen God visible for all to see.

God Renews Us

The dawn glows with beauty. As the sun begins to meet the eastern horizon, the first rays of light and energy shoot upward, dispelling darkness and warming the ground. The earth shakes off the stillness and quiet of the night. Animals arise from their burrows and begin to forage for food. Flowers bend toward the light and open to their source of life. As the light grows brighter and the warmth more intense, the world awakens from its rest and life begins anew. Dawn happens every day. We can't always view the golden beams of the sun or feel its warming rays, yet they always renew the world.

Nature has a special way of exhibiting God's daily renewal. Its dramatic effects vividly touch our senses. Without the drama or vivid imagery, God still renews each of us. Each time we pray the Lord's Prayer we say, "Give us this day our daily bread." We ask God to renew and sustain us with whatever we need. Ever watchful and vigilant, God gives us our daily bread and much more besides.

God renews the human race most powerfully through his great mercy. As humans we are finite, incomplete, fractured and sinful. Each day we struggle to live in a world which often does not appreciate our presence. We have ecstasies and failures. Most days are relatively uneventful. The humanness which is our lot sometimes weighs us down; it seems like an overwhelming, even crushing burden. Often God seems far away, and we fear that the refreshment we need will never come.

Whether we see it or not, God does renew all people each day. The author of the Book of Lamentations stated the reality, "The steadfast love of the Lord never ceases, his mercies never come to an end; they are new every morning; great is his faithfulness" (3:22-23). Each day we receive a new chance from our God. It is not something we deserve or a prize earned from our previous day's work. No, God's daily renewal of mercy is a gift, and like all good gifts, it costs nothing. The recipient only needs to accept it.

The daily renewal of nature cannot compare with the renewal found each day in humanity, God's greatest creation. The beauty of nature and the magnificence of each new day is a special gift from God. But the renewal in the human spirit can be even more beautiful and powerful to one who has felt the burdens of life lifted by the gentle yet powerful hand of the Lord. Tranquillity enters where chaos reigned, and the human soul once again tastes peace.

St. Augustine wrote in his *Confessions*, "Our hearts are restless until they rest in you" (Book 1). Like Augustine of old, many people today mistakenly search in the things of this world for the rest that only God can give. But the renewal which God gives each day is interior. The good news for us is that the faithfulness of God renews us each day. Let us open ourselves to the mercy which God offers. As the dawn breaks on our world today, let us find the light and warmth of the Lord, a gift which only God can give.

God Speaks to Us

Love through Death

Love illuminates the scene of Christ's passion and death, although it might seem to clash with the bloody scene on Calvary. Love impelled Jesus to offer his life for us. Christ's eternal love for us shone in his outstretched arms on the cross.

St. Paul's hymn in Philippians 2:6-11 reveals to us the power of Jesus' love. What else but love would induce the incarnate God to suffer such a bloody death? St. Paul wrote that Jesus, "Though he was in the form of God, did not count equality with God a thing to be grasped, but emptied himself, taking the form of a servant, being born in the likeness of men. And being found in human form he humbled himself and became obedient unto death, even death on a cross" (2:6-9). Jesus' death ransomed us for life. The cross weighed Jesus down with bitter pain. But his ultimate sacrifice bestows life on us. The cross confers life and salvation on us, through Jesus' great love.

Jesus' outstretched arms on the cross invite us to love in return. "This is my commandment, that you love one another as I have loved you" (Jn 15:12). Although we often fail to live up to this commandment, we know that God's eternal love pursues us. Jesus continues to pour out his love on us, even though we don't deserve it. With all our brokenness and shortcomings, Jesus still opens his arms for us. "But God shows his love for us in that while we were yet sinners Christ died for us" (Rom 5:8). Christ's love for his people even shatters the chains of death.

Even though it brought death to Jesus, the crucifixion brings life to those who follow him. We puzzle over how life can come from death, yet the paradox of Christ's death in order to bring us life enlivens our faith. We know that the joy of Easter will disperse the sorrow of Good Friday. So even the sorrow in Jesus' passion and death means joy for Christians. Christ's love radiated even from the cross. Jesus prayed for his executioners, "Father, forgive them; for they know not what they do" (Lk 23:34a). Likewise Jesus gave hope to the repentant thief, "Truly I say to you, today you will be with me in paradise" (Lk 23:43). With Jesus as our example and guide, let us strive to show love through death, to reach out and touch someone despite the pain. Our call as Christians demands our commitment. From Calvary Jesus invites our response.

God's Love

What can separate us from the love of God? In chapter 8 of his Letter to the Romans, St. Paul reassures us that nothing can take God's love away from us. God's everlasting love always surrounds us, and it costs absolutely nothing.

Two images come to mind when reflecting on Romans 8:31-39. First, I think of the sun with its warm rays penetrating into the deepest recesses of the earth. Nothing can escape the sun's power or extinguish its energy. Second, I think of a single light bulb in the middle of a barren and darkened room. When the light shines, nothing can escape it. The light shines on everything in the room, beaming life into the gloom.

But the sun and the light bulb only dimly reflect

the immensity of God's love. It permeates even the darkest places of people's hearts. God's love cannot be diminished or extinguished in any way, but surrounds us totally. We cannot escape its effect.

The love of God burns within us so deeply, yet today's world entices us to forget about God. We can hide from the sun and the light. We can turn our back and hide in a dark place, or build walls around ourselves. Likewise, we may try to shun God's love. Material goods, personal relationships and secularization can build up barriers to keep God's love out. Yet, even as the sun's rays beating on one's back beckon a person to turn to the light and warmth, so too does God's love invite us to a change of heart. When God's love fills our lives, it asks us to rid ourselves of those things which we have turned into idols. The process may sear our hearts, but life with Jesus fills us with joy.

We know that God's love never abandons us, but we may lack the faith to act upon that belief. If it seems that the flame of God's love has flickered out, remember the words of St. Paul, "For I am sure that neither death, nor life, neither angels, nor principalities, nor things present, nor things to come, nor powers, nor height, nor depth, nor anything else in all creation, will be able to separate us from the love of

God in Christ Jesus, our Lord" (Rom 8:38-39). Turn to the sun, refuse to flee the light, and receive the reward of everlasting life.

Thy Kingdom Come

The one prayer that all Christians accept is the Lord's Prayer. It is prayed in slightly different forms, but it is universal because Jesus himself taught us this prayer. Every day we pray, "thy kingdom come," but do we realize what that means? Do we know how that statement can affect our daily lives?

In praying, "thy kingdom come," we pray that God's reign will come to this world. But isn't God's kingdom already here? Doesn't the Spirit of God pervade our entire existence? The answer is yes, without a doubt. Then what do we pray for when we say, "thy kingdom come"?

Possibly the answer can be found in Matthew 10:34-11:1. In this difficult passage Jesus told his apostles that he has not come to bring peace, but division. He has come to set children and parents at odds. And Jesus continued, "He who loves father or mother more than me is not worthy of me; and he who loves son or daughter more than me is not worthy of me; and he who does not take his cross and follow me is not worthy of me" (10:37-38). How can this be? Why would our loving God bring division? Why does Jesus seem so harsh?

Jesus' words seems rough and out of character, but they teach us an important and valuable lesson. Jesus warns us that nothing can come before the kingdom. If peace hinders the growth of God's kingdom, then division is better. If one's mother or father, children or spouse obstructs the growth of the kingdom, then one must confront that person. The kingdom must take first priority. Nothing can come between ourselves and God's kingdom. If it does, then we have lost the path and we need to turn back to God.

Jesus told us of the rewards for those who cherish the kingdom above all else. If we welcome the prophets of God, we will receive a prophet's reward. If we welcome a holy person, then we will receive a holy person's reward. If we give a cup of cold water to a lowly person, our reward cannot be measured. Placing God first will shower us with all that we need to find eternal life with our Creator.

"Thy kingdom come" challenges us to keep our priorities straight. With all the activities of our life and all the demands made on us, we can easily stray in the wrong direction. Let Jesus' words inspire us to follow the Lord and fully live the Christian life. Then we will know the truth of God and this truth will set us free.

Say Yes to God

Imagine, if you can, the scene that day when the angel Gabriel came to Mary, the daughter of Ann and Joachim. Theologians today tell us that Mary was probably 14 years old. God sent an angel with a special invitation to a humble virgin, living in an equally humble home and village. Gabriel stated, "Hail, O favored one, the Lord is with you!" (Lk 1:28). Mary was confused but Gabriel continued, "Do not be afraid, Mary, for you have found favor with God...you will conceive in your womb and bear a son, and you shall call his name Jesus" (Lk 1:30b-31).

In a matter of moments Mary's whole life changed. We can relate to the anxiety she must have felt. She was engaged to Joseph, a good and upright man. She probably dreamed of their family life together. I am sure that Mary did not dream of power, wealth and prestige. This would not have been possible nor desired by one such as Mary. Yet, she certainly dreamed of the future as we all do.

But how did Mary answer the request of God's messenger? She did not fight, argue or run away. She simply asked how such a miraculous happening was possible. She did not persist in disbelief as Zechariah did. Rather, she accepted God's invitation with her famous fiat, "I am the servant of the Lord. Let it be done to me as you say" (Lk 1:38). From that day on, Mary never looked back. She knew her purpose and mission in life.

Few of us will ever be asked to change our lives as radically as Mary. Along the road of life the Lord invites most of us to join him in various works that foster the kingdom of God. I suspect that we often avoid many of God's invitations. We might excuse ourselves by saying that we are too busy or the time is not right. The call may urge us to help others or to change our attitude. The call may invite us to join some cause, or encourage us to a new way of life. When we spurn the invitation of the Lord, we miss the opportunity of a lifetime. Fortunately for us, God calls continually and never gives up on us.

God will call today. What will we answer? Let us take the attitude of Mary and see ourselves as servants of the Creator, our God. Let us say yes to the Lord this day.

I Want to See

"Day by day, day by day, O dear Lord, three things I pray—to see thee more clearly, love thee more dearly, follow thee more nearly day by day." These words from the popular musical *Godspell* tell us much about our life as a daily opportunity to see, love and follow the Lord more fully.

St. Luke's Gospel recounts how Jesus healed a blind man (18:35-43). This account shows us how we can see, love and follow the Lord. The simple scene engages our attention. A blind man crouched along the road and heard a group of people talking excitedly as they passed by. He asked what was happening. When he discovered Jesus was leading the crowed, the blind man cried out, "Jesus, Son of David, have mercy on me." The people told him to be quiet, but he only cried out the louder. Jesus summoned the man and asked, "What do you want me to do for you?" "Lord, let me receive my sight," the man begged. Ever compassionate, Jesus cured the blind man. The man could then see clearly.

Why did Jesus have compassion on this man and cure him? Jesus met him by chance. Yet, something drew Jesus' attention—the man's faith. He wanted to love God more dearly. Jesus sensed this and cured the man. Jesus said to him, "Receive your sight; your faith has made you well" (18:42). The man's faith gave him the ability to love and prompted Jesus to cure him. Luke tells us that the man began to follow Jesus. The man wanted to be near the Lord. Jesus had responded to his need and the man, in turn, wanted to show his appreciation.

This story in St. Luke's Gospel challenges us. It asks us to see more clearly. This means throwing off the blinders which narrow our vision. We must be able to see God in all forms and all places. If we refuse to look, then we miss opportunities to see God. To see more clearly gives us the whole picture, not only one limited view. We need to love more dearly as the blind man did. We show our love in prayer, action and reflection. Becoming more God-centered challenges us and entails the work of a lifetime. But we need to start now, not tomorrow. True love of God leads us to selfless service and caring for others. We need to keep our eyes fixed on the ultimate goal of our lives, which is following the way of the Lord. Whatever we do or wherever we go, union with God beckons us as the final goal of our lives. Following God's law and walking in his way starts us on a path that leads to union with God.

The blind man of Luke's Gospel has shown us

in a simple way the method that we can use to find God. When we love God, then we can begin to see all things more clearly and follow the Lord more nearly. The blind man had faith. We too must show our belief in God's presence. It will lead us to greater joy in our lives day by day.

Jesus Knocks at the Door of our Heart

A popular work of art shows Jesus in a garden facing the door to a small cottage. At first glance the scene appears normal, but a closer look reveals an important detail. The door facing Jesus has no knob. The Lord is knocking. The artist has expressed the truth of a popular Scripture passage. The Book of Revelation states, "Behold, I stand at the door and knock; if any one hears my voice and opens the door, I will come in to him and eat with him, and he with me" (Rev 3:20). Jesus is knocking at the door of our heart. The door has no knob, for it can only be opened from within. We alone hold the key. Jesus can knock and ask to enter, but we must let him in. God always invites us into his presence and never forces it upon us.

We know most certainly that God freely invites us. I suspect that most of us could honestly say that when the Lord has knocked we have opened our hearts. On one level this may be true. We call ourselves people of faith. We say we are the Church, the people of God. God dwells among us. But on another, deeper level, I wonder if we truly do allow God to enter. This level concerns our fellow men and women. Do they have as easy access to our person as God does?

God often knocks on the door of our heart each day. When we are engrossed in our job and a co-worker stops by to say hello, to ask for advice or our opinion, we can hear God knocking. When we drive home in bumper-to-bumper traffic, we can hear God knocking, asking for our patience. When we come home after a long and frustrating day, we can hear God knocking in the requests of our spouse and our children. When a relative or friend writes or calls asking for our time, we can hear God knocking again. In these moments do we welcome God as freely, or do we protect our private space and refuse to answer God's call? We can't solve all the problems or meet all the needs in our immediate world. But we can provide a place for God in the many ways that God comes to us. Remember Jesus' promise in Matthew's Gospel, "As you did it to one of the least of these my brethren, you did it to me" (Mt 25:40b).

When we open our hearts to others in welcome, we open our hearts to God.

When we allow God access to our hearts, we will find ourselves transformed. The world brightens, our brokenness heals and interruptions—whether from co-workers, children, friends or a vagrant begging for spare change—become graced moments. If we allow Jesus in, then he will dine with us and transform our world.

God will knock today. How will we respond? Let us open the door of our hearts to God. Let us find a permanent place for the Lord in our lives and in each day to come.

The Word of God

Words can harm and words can heal. Whether printed or spoken, words can inspire or anger us. Words can carry us to new heights of hope or they can cast us into the depths of despair.

Scripture abounds in vivid and powerful images of the Word of God. We read in Isaiah, "For as the rain and the snow come down from heaven, and return not thither but water the earth, making it bring forth and sprout, giving seed to the sower and bread to the eater, so shall my word be that goes forth from my mouth; it shall not return to me empty, but it shall accomplish that which I purpose" (55:10-11). God's word accomplishes its mission, just as the rain does. Rain waters the earth, allowing nature to bud forth. So too, the Word of God waters and nourishes us, allowing the seed of faith which God plants in our hearts to blossom. The rains return to the heavens after they have nurtured the earth. The Word of God returns to our Creator after it has fed us for our spiritual journey.

God's word demands a receptive heart. If you watch rain fall from the sky, you will notice that much of the water nurtures nothing, but runs off and is lost. Storm drains swallow the rain that falls on streets and sidewalks, and funnel it to a river or the ocean. Only the rain which falls on prepared soil can produce the fruits of the land. Similarly the word of God can only be effective when we allow it to permeate our being. How can this happen? We need to allow God's word, the two-edged sword, to pierce our heart and soul so that God's ever-flowing love can find room in us.

The words we speak, the words we hear and the words we read have power to build up or tear down. The power of God's word in our life highlights this for us. In Scripture Jesus gives us words for prayer in the Our Father (Mt 6:9b-13). St. John tells us that "The Word became flesh and dwelt among us" (Jn 1:14a). The power of words constantly impacts our lives. We communicate in words and God has revealed himself in words. God's Word came to show us the way to the Father. Words can build up the reign of God in our world. God has given us the imagery of Isaiah and the life of Jesus to show us the way. May we be receptive to the words which we encounter this day.

God Comes to Us

Easter

"He saw and believed" (Jn 20:8b). With these words, the Gospel tells us about St. John's experience of the resurrection. What did he see that made him believe? He saw the wrappings and the stone that had been rolled away. Possibly he saw some vision or aura of light. John saw the empty tomb. Jesus' body was not there. What had happened? Had the soldiers taken it? Had he been raised? Was he alive? I am sure that many ideas crossed John's mind, but what he actually saw that day was the emptiness. The emptiness allowed him to believe.

Like the rest of us, John was a busy person. He had obligations as a fisherman. His daily activities kept his mind occupied. The emptiness of the tomb must have struck him powerfully. John was busy, but he made room for the Lord. He gave Jesus the chance to enter his life. The power of the resurrection could only touch John's life because he was ready to accept the Risen Lord.

Our modern century presses us for time. The day's demands hurry us along the road of life. Time slips by before we can write that letter we've been putting off, or make that call to a loved one. Work often swallows our time for relaxation. Where does that leave the Lord? Do we give him a chance to come into our lives? Or does our busy schedule shut God out, too?

The resurrection cannot make an impact on our lives if we don't leave ourselves open to it. The empty tomb which allowed John to see and believe beckons us as well. It calls us to empty ourselves so that God may enter. Easter challenges us to find time and space for God so that we too can see and believe. When we allow the risen Lord into our lives, he will transform them.

Thanksgiving

We celebrate a special day of Thanksgiving each year. But we need to be grateful every day of our lives. Thanksgiving is a life long process of re-membrance. We remember our faith, family and friends. We remember the God who gave us life and sustains us with our daily bread. We remember that we are creatures, born for different purposes, yet all destined to return to the Creator from whom we came and for whom we live.

But thanksgiving must go beyond a mere thank you. A word of thanks can grace our day. But we mustn't stop at words. Thanksgiving demands our service. It calls us to give our life back to our God who has given us all things from the beginning. Thanksgiving must be a way of life which gives glory to God by giving to others as God has given to us.

On Thanksgiving Day we spread the table with turkey, ham, bread, vegetables, yams and pie for dessert. We might toast our fortune, small though it may be. We gather with family and friends. It is a good time to renew family bonds and to relax with our friends. We thank them for their support and presence. We give thanks to God for the abundance which flows from the heavens.

Still, with all the beauty that this day brings, it lacks something if our gratitude ends at sunset. An attitude of thanksgiving to God and others should mark our way of life. But how can we be grateful in the midst of difficulty, economic setbacks and a society which doesn't seem to care about us? Changing our attitudes might be a start. Many of us think that God or the world owes us something. We might rage at life's unfairness when we don't have what we think we need. What did we do to deserve such abuse? We probably did nothing. Nevertheless, having a victim's attitude can make us demanding and selfish. Instead, we need to recall that all of life is a gift. God denies us nothing, although human beings might be unjust.

Thanksgiving gives us the key to a happy life. If we can show others that we care and are grateful for their presence, then we show our thankfulness to God. Their presence is the presence of God to us. Let us be thankful each day for all that God has given us. Let us display that thankfulness to all, showing a true spirit of Christian love.

New Beginnings

When the month of December shows up on the calendar, we realize that time has nudged us into another Advent. This season brings hope and a chance for renewal. It gives us an opportunity to grow in our relationship with God.

At first glance it might seem strange to think of Advent as a time of new beginnings. The bare trees stand stark against the gray winter sky. Cold weather blows in and the longer nights chase the sun away. It seems like a period of endings, not beginnings. Yet just as darkness seems to triumph, it's beaten back and begins to wane. The winter equinox signals the rebirth of light. As Scripture says, "The night is far gone, the day is at hand. Let us then cast off the works of darkness and put on the armor of light" (Rom 13:12). New beginnings happen when the light shines forth, not only in our world, but in our attitudes.

Advent can help us re-evaluate our attitudes toward others and their ways of thinking. When we reject out of hand the thoughts and experiences of others, we miss the opportunity to expand our vision. We may not agree, but by listening we can broaden our outlook and grow. We cannot live in this world alone. We need others and the richness they bring to our lives.

New beginnings happen in our work as well. We can renew our commitments to others and to important works. The Christian life calls us to service and Advent can call us to a new sense of service in our life. We can renew or begin personal relationships. We have the opportunity to cast off our selfishness which isolates us from others, and begin to be more hospitable in welcoming others into our life. We'll probably be surprised by all the grace and renewal we can attain merely by allowing God to enter our hearts through the lives of others.

New beginnings always challenge us. They require us to stretch and to look beyond ourselves. They may bring some pain, but without the pain we can't grow. If we listen, we'll hear God challenging us almost daily to broaden our view and to open ourselves more fully. As a time of hope, Advent is a time to find a new beginning in attitude, in word and in action. Advent is a time to seek peace in a broken world. May our new beginnings bring us closer to God and to God's people.

Finding the Light— A Christmas Reflection

Picture yourself in a forest. As night falls, clouds cover the moon and stars. The darkness lends an atmosphere of gloom to the scene. You grope your way around in the dark. You finally remember that you brought a candle and matches with you.

Pulling the candle from your pocket, you light it and place it on a nearby tree stump. What does one notice from the candle? First, the light of the candle radiates in all directions. It goes to all things at all times. The light of the candle brings warmth and direction. We can use the candle to find our way. The light of the candle adds clarity as well. Not only can we see the way but we can better recognize the danger spots that might lurk ahead. We can see more clearly which way to go. Finally the light of the candle dispels fear. We may fear the danger which lurks in the darkness. But the light of the candle dispels fear and brings us hope.

About two thousand years ago the Hebrew people lived in darkness, waiting for the Messiah. The light of the world had not yet come. Even though darkness reigned, the people had hope. As Isaiah the prophet says, "The people who walked in darkness have seen a great light" (9:2). The people were waiting for the light to enter the world, the one whom they would call, "Wonderful Counselor, Mighty God, Everlasting Father, Prince of Peace" (Is 9:6). With the arrival of the promised one, the Christ, the light entered the world.

Jesus came as the light of the world, and he brought what the light of the candle brings. First, he brought himself, and he is none other than love. Like the light, the love of Christ radiates in all directions to all peoples. As St. Paul tells us in his Letter to the Romans (cf. 8:35-39), no one can escape from the love of Christ except the person who rejects God's love. The light which is Jesus warms us. If we are hurting, sorrowful or in need of comfort, the light of Christ will sustain us. The light assists us in all our needs. The light of Jesus brings us direction and clarity. Guided by the Lord, we know better which way to go and we can avoid the pitfalls and detours which hinder our progress back to God. Finally, the light of Christ brings us hope while dispelling fear. Jesus, the light, does this by rekindling the spark of faith, which is a gift of God. Faith dispels fear. The light which is Jesus brings everything that the light of the candle brings but more, for Jesus is the light of the whole world.

Jesus' birth brings us hope. Jesus freely chose to come to our world. Jesus chose to become human, like us in all things but sin. Jesus chose to suffer and so redeem us. Jesus was born that first Christmas day. What we celebrate at Christmas is the re-birth of light into our world. With Jesus not physically present, it might seem difficult to see the light. Thus we are challenged to become the light of Christ for others. We must bring love where none exists, and warmth where sorrow reigns. We must be willing to give direction to others. We must dispel fear and raise hope. Let us this Christmas bring love, warmth and direction to others. Let us rekindle the light of the Lord in our lives and share our warmth with others. Let the spirit of Christmas live in our hearts today and every day of our lives.

Pauline BOOKS & MEDIA

ALASKA
750 West 5th Ave., Anchorage, AK 99501; 907-272-8183

CALIFORNIA
3908 Sepulveda Blvd., Culver City, CA 90230; 310-397-8676
5945 Balboa Ave., San Diego, CA 92111; 619-565-9181
46 Geary Street, San Francisco, CA 94108; 415-781-5180

FLORIDA
145 S.W. 107th Ave., Miami, FL 33174; 305-559-6715

HAWAII
1143 Bishop Street, Honolulu, HI 96813; 808-521-2731

ILLINOIS
172 North Michigan Ave., Chicago, IL 60601; 312-346-4228

LOUISIANA
4403 Veterans Memorial Blvd., Metairie, LA 70006; 504-887-7631

MASSACHUSETTS
50 St. Paul's Ave., Jamaica Plain, Boston, MA 02130; 617-522-8911
Rte. 1, 885 Providence Hwy., Dedham, MA 02026; 617-326-5385

MISSOURI
9804 Watson Rd., St. Louis, MO 63126; 314-965-3512

NEW JERSEY
561 U.S. Route 1, Wick Plaza, Edison, NJ 08817; 908-572-1200

NEW YORK
150 East 52nd Street, New York, NY 10022; 212-754-1110
78 Fort Place, Staten Island, NY 10301; 718-447-5071

OHIO
2105 Ontario Street (at Prospect Ave.), Cleveland, OH 44115; 216-621-9427

PENNSYLVANIA
Northeast Shopping Center, 9171-A Roosevelt Blvd. (between Grant Ave. & Welsh Rd.), Philadelphia, PA 19114; 215-676-9494

SOUTH CAROLINA
243 King Street, Charleston, SC 29401; 803-577-0175

TENNESSEE
4811 Poplar Ave., Memphis, TN 38117 901-761-2987

TEXAS
114 Main Plaza, San Antonio, TX 78205; 210-224-8101

VIRGINIA
1025 King Street, Alexandria, VA 22314; 703-549-3806

CANADA
3022 Dufferin Street, Toronto, Ontario, Canada M6B 3T5; 416-781-9131